THE COURAGE TO CARE

SUZI SMEED & TERENCE J. QUINN

connorcourt
PUBLISHING

Published in 2023 by Connor Court Publishing Pty Ltd.

Copyright © Suzi Smeed & Terence J. Quinn

All rights reserved. Not to be reproduced without the permission of the Copyright holders.

Connor Court Publishing Pty Ltd.
PO Box 7257
Redland Bay QLD 4165
sales@connorcourt.com
www.connorcourt.com

ISBN: 9781922815422 (paperback)
         9781922815453 (hardback)

Cover Design by Ian James

Printed in Australia.

"You ask how you might help the cause of Jewish memory. The only thing I can suggest is to continue what you have been doing: writing and speaking in order to educate those who are not yet aware."

Elie Wiesel, Holocaust survivor and Nobel Peace Prize-winner

PRAISE FOR *THE COURAGE TO CARE*

I have known Suzi Smeed for many years. Her book is the bittersweet story of a child, a holocaust survivor, who learned how to love rather than hate. I like the fact that she is now dedicated to teaching new generations that same vital lesson.
David Kirby KC, former Justice of the Supreme Court of NSW.

Suzi Smeed has done an extraordinary and courageous job via her memoir of the Hungarian Holocaust. Not only did she survive the terrifying trauma and create a new life in Australia with its own story of triumph, but she also alerts us to the continuing cultural concern about the growth of anti-Semitism in Australia. In this candid and compelling memoir, she reminds us why we must embrace that responsibility. For someone to chronicle her experiences, as Suzi has done, demonstrates immense moral strength,
Alan Jones AO, broadcaster and former Wallabies Coach.

Against the background of the beating of the war drums in Europe, Suzi Smeed, one of the last survivors of the holocaust, tells her story of her escape from the gas ovens and the making of a new life in Australia. This is the history and the true memoir of an indomitable woman.
Ian Callinan AC, Former Australian High Court Judge, novelist and playwright.

This is a riveting account about the survival of a little girl during the ethnic cleansing of her community by brutal savages. Suzi's words convey deep conviction, emotional intensity, intelligence, and learning. She is the epitome of human triumph over evil, not only surviving - but thriving and making a difference. I am honoured to know her, and proud to call her my dear and very close friend.

Brigitte Gabriel, Founder & Chairman, ACT For America

Suzi Smeed is someone I've had the pleasure of knowing for some years. Whilst I was aware of her Hungarian Holocaust background, it didn't prepare me for the ongoing and heart-breaking series of dramas that unfold in this marvellous read. I know Suzi as an intellectual, loving and nurturing human being. That Suzi has become this person despite those terrible experiences speaks to the resilience and capacity of this amazing lady. Suzi's book is a must read.

Llew O'Brien, Federal Member for Wide Bay, Deputy Speaker for the House of Representatives.

The lessons of the Holocaust must never be forgotten. We are so grateful to Suzi for her personal and eloquently-told story, and for her passionate commitment to educating future generations. This story is Suzi's legacy and a shining tribute to the 568,000 Hungarian Jews whose lives were cruelly ended by evil.

Jason Steinberg, Chairman, Queensland Holocaust Museum and Education Centre.

DEDICATION

This memoir is dedicated to my mother Erzsebet, my grandparents Jeno and Irma, and all who perished in the Shoah.

CONTENTS

Praise for *The Courage to Care*	v
Dedication	vii
Contents	viii
Introduction – HE Amir Maimon, Ambassador of the State of Israel to Australia	xi
Prologue – *A small piece in the stained-glass window depicting the Shoah*	xiii
Part One: 40 A.D. to 1943	1
Chapter 1 – *Jews: The scapegoats of history*	3
Chapter 2 – *A gnarled family tree*	9
Chapter 3 – *Courtship amidst chaos*	13
Chapter 4 – *War and a wedding*	19
Illustrations	25
Part 2: 1944–1945	31
Chapter 5 – *The hounds of hell*	33
Chapter 6 – *Forced into slavery*	37
Chapter 7 – *The gates of hell*	41
Chapter 8 – *Deportation Zone V*	45
Chapter 9 – *Staring death in the face*	47
Chapter 10 – *The safe house on Saletrom Street*	53
Chapter 11 – *Heroes and villains*	59
Chapter 12 – *Ticket to freedom*	65
Chapter 13 – *A family under siege*	71

Chapter 14 – *The Hungarian Hamlet* — 77
Chapter 15 – *A new nightmare* — 87
Chapter 16 – *The search for 'Zsuzsiki'* — 97
Illustrations — 103

Part 3: 1945 – present — 117
Chapter 17 – *Saved from the secret police* — 119
Chapter 18 – *Goodnight Vienna* — 127
Chapter 19 – *Viva Vivaldi* — 133
Chapter 20 – *G'day Australia!* — 139
Chapter 21 – *Lessons in life* — 145
Chapter 22 – *Revolution and a family tragedy* — 149
Chapter 23 – *My Jewish awakening* — 153
Chapter 24 – *London calling, and marriage mismatch No 1* — 159
Chapter 25 – *Innocence* — 165
Chapter 26 – *Mismatch No 2 and a heart-wrenching tragedy* — 171
Chapter 27 – *Suzanne of The Strand* — 177
Chapter 28 – *The air-con guy and the redhead* — 183
Chapter 29 – *Mum & Dad: love, life and loss* — 191
Chapter 30 – *How I gained the courage to care* — 201
Illustrations — 209

Conclusion – Never, ever again — 223
Chronology of the Hungarian Holocaust — 231
Acknowledgements — 237
Sources used in this memoir — 241
About the authors — 243

INTRODUCTION

A few months after assuming my duties as Ambassador to Australia, I asked Suzi Smeed to visit Canberra to mark Yom HaShoah (Holocaust Remembrance Day) at the Embassy. I had invited a number of guests to the Embassy Residence to hear her speak. It was a diverse audience; young and old, with members of the local community and diplomats from at least a dozen countries.

I will always remember that occasion, because every person in that room, regardless of age and background, was utterly captivated by Suzi's story and her message. For weeks afterward, I continued to receive appreciative feedback from those who were there that night. It was a testament to Suzi's gift for making history resonate with people, and her ability to bridge the divide between the present and the past. Her words made a profound impact.

The task of Holocaust education is so important because the lessons from history remain urgent. It requires a special type of person to act as custodian of this difficult chapter of our past, and to be willing and able to share it in a way that resonates with contemporary audiences.

Suzi is precisely such a person. Her vivacious personality, sharp sense of humour, and compelling story of survival transcend the boundaries of age, culture and faith. Her words speak directly to our common humanity.

I thank Suzi for her friendship and for the invaluable work she does in educating Australians about the Holocaust – and I congratulate her and Terence on the publication of this important book.

Amir Maimon, Israeli Ambassador of the State of Israel to Australia

PROLOGUE

A small piece in the stained-glass window depicting the Shoah

"There is no doubt that this persecution of Jews in Hungary and their expulsion from enemy territory is probably the greatest and most horrible crime ever committed in the whole history of the world ..."

That is how Winston Churchill condemned the relentless Nazi killing machine that transported vast numbers of Hungarian Jews to the death camps at Auschwitz-Birkenau between 15 May and 9 July 1944. Estimates of the total toll vary from 423,271 to 437,402. What is certain is that most were murdered on arrival.

That is just fifty-six days. It was, scholars agree, the quickest mass deportation carried out during the entire Holocaust. A grotesque tribute to German efficiency on a monstrous scale. Every day, four trains of the Hungarian Sate Railway (MAV), each carrying three thousand Jews, would leave Hungary for Ozwiecim, the small town in Poland where the industrialised extermination centre known as *Konzentrationslager Auschwitz* was sited. A total of 147 transports. By the end of the war, one third of all the people murdered at Auschwitz were Jews from every corner of Hungary.

Here are the mechanics of mass murder: the rail track was specially built to accommodate the huge volume of Hungarian human cargo; each train had a steam engine and between thirty and fifty poorly ventilated cattle cars, with up to one hundred men, women and children herded into each ten-metre-long wagon; they had already been brutalised, rounded up in ghettoes and robbed of their possessions; the average transportation took between three and five days and the Jewish prisoners had only the water and food they had with them, and a bucket in the corner of each wagon as a toilet; typically, eighty per cent of new arrivals at Auschwitz-Birkenau would be classed as "Ballastexistenz" (a waste of space, or dead weight), and earmarked for immediate murder. Those sad souls were then stripped naked and packed into the gas chambers, up to three thousand at a time. The Zyklon B gas would kill them within six or seven minutes.

Jewish prisoners conscripted into slave worker groups called Sonderkommando then stripped the bodies of gold dental fillings, jewellery and even women's hair before they were burnt in pits, on pyres or in large crematoria. Five of the latter contained up to fifteen ovens that were kept going non-stop, day and night. The ashes of the victims were then dumped in nearby rivers, strewn in the fields as fertiliser or used as landfill.

Among them were Jeno Halasz and his wife Irma. My grandparents. But for a miracle, my mother and I would have been killed alongside them. More of that later. Jeno and Irma had lived all their lives in Papa, a small, historic town in Veszprem County near the Austrian border, about 120 kilometres west of Budapest towards Austria.

Papa was a peaceful, prosperous place where Jews had lived in relative harmony since 1748 ... that is, until 19 March 1944 – the day the Germans occupied Hungary and SS Obersturmbannfuhrer Adolf Eichmann, notorious as the 'architect of the Holocaust', and his Judenkommando, arrived in Budapest with one objective: make Hungary *Judenfrei* – free of Jews. At that point, the country had a Jewish population of around 800,000. Significantly, it was the first time Eichmann had left the safety of his Berlin HQ to personally oversee his hellish schemes in another country.

There are key moments in the life of every nation that provide a turning point, and this was one of them. Up to then, Hungary was considered a comparatively safe haven for Jews, largely because its alignment with the Axis powers. Indeed, many Jews in other European countries had flocked there during the first few years of the war to escape the vast and diabolical conspiracy – the Endlosung der Judenfrage, or Final Solution to the Jewish Question – designed to exterminate millions of people because of their race and religion. Hungary had the most intact Jewish community left standing in Europe – the last to succumb to Nazism.

But when the Hungarian government renounced its support for the Axis powers following Germany's disastrous invasion of Russia, the Nazis retaliated by invading its former ally. Despite the tide of war having turned strongly against them – the D-Day landings were just weeks away, and Hitler would kill himself within a year – the Nazis remained bewilderingly fixated on annihilating Jews.

Meanwhile, Eichmann launched a barrage of new anti-Semitic laws and decrees, each designed to humiliate Jews, restrict their lives and strip them of their property and possessions.

In mid-May, deportations to the death camps began.

I was less than two years old when the German Tiger tanks rumbled into Hungary, and thus mercifully oblivious to the world-changing events happening around me and the terror that continued to turn my family's lives upside down for several more years. After the war, when my parents and I were finally safe as refugees in Australia, the mix of disbelief and relief to some extent muted our contemplation of the horrific experiences we had endured, first at the hands of the Nazis and then from the so-called Red Army 'liberators'.

It was never discussed in any detail, but I would listen in horror to the gut-wrenching experiences of friends and neighbours. It has taken me more than seven decades to process and fully piece together the heinous and yet sometimes heart-warming episodes that punctuated my early childhood, episodes that included escaping certain death from the unholy alliance of German Nazis and Hungarian fascists.

A great number of scholarly works and poignant memoirs have been written about the Holocaust, many of them from actual survivors of the ghettoes and the camps. Their testimony is first-hand; they speak from personal experiences that were as unimaginable as they were unspeakable. They expose the dark evil that was visited upon the friends and family who were murdered, while shining a bright light on the courage and inner spirit of those who survived.

With this memoir, I do not, cannot, set out to emulate them. Why? Because I was luckier than they were; because I narrowly escaped being sent to Auschwitz, and because I was too young to understand why the nightmare had been visited on us. As a result, much of what I write about is second-hand, hearsay from family members and others who were there, in Budapest, as war and attempted genocide raged about them in 1944.

These were people who also shook and shivered in dark corners as the Russians bombed and besieged the Hungarian capital in 1945, determined to drive the Nazis from the blasted sewers and debris-strewn streets of that once magnificent city. Astonishingly, most of the horrific events I write about are contained in one twelve-month period – from mid-March 1944 to early February 1945 when the German forces in Budapest surrendered. During that short time, more than 570,000 Hungarian Jews were murdered out of the 800,000 living there before the war.

Researching this project opened a Pandora's Box of bittersweet thoughts and emotions that were unsettling and disturbed my sleep. Some of them were nostalgic and familiar – blurry memories of my comfortable family life in Budapest, stimulated by family photographs and letters. Other episodes were (and still are) shocking and searing – like the time I was abandoned in an orphanage while my parents hid in the crawl space of our apartment in Budapest; and the sight of a woman being brutally raped by a Russian soldier. Yet more images flicker in my mind telling the story of our escape to Australia and my gradual awakening to the horrors we left behind.

The shadowy figure of Samu Stern, my mother's 'bacsi' (a Hungarian term meaning a close friend of the family known as 'uncle' but not blood related) also looms large. Stern was a prominent Jewish leader forced to engage in a deadly dance with Adolf Eichmann and his cronies following the German occupation. He also played a pivotal role in my family narrative.

I've included a fair amount of big-picture, broad-sweep historical detail in the following narrative, partly to provide context to my family story, and partly because I had not known much of it before my research began. My eyes were opened to many things, some personal, others relating to the senseless brutality unleashed on the country of my birth.

Following my family's escape from communist oppression in 1948, I returned to Budapest twice – in 1964 when the deadening Soviet influence made for a depressing experience, and again in 2002 when I revisited many of the places that would have been familiar to my parents and met some of the people still living who knew them.

Here, I should warn unsuspecting readers that it is acceptable practice in memoirs to combine characters, rename characters, omit events, fictionalise dialogue, compress or combine events, and otherwise manipulate time in the interest of telling a more compelling story. But – and it is a big 'but' – writers must still commit to telling the essential truth. I have tried very hard to do that here. To tell *my* truth.

And, while much of the wider historical details about the war, the (mostly) men who waged it and the horrors of the Holocaust I use to provide context and background to my story is well-chronicled (albeit many published accounts differ on exact details such as numbers or names of places), some other characters and events have come from research, and I have 'shaped' them to enrich the narrative. I've also taken inspiration and adapted details of the experiences of various Hungarian survivors whose nightmare stories and innate courage still haunt me.

The eighteenth-century statesman and philosopher Edmund Burke said: 'The triumph of evil required for good men to do nothing.' Sadly, I spent my first seventy years doing just that – nothing; or at least very little with regard to confronting those horrors from my childhood, that heinous inhumanity to man. But in my seventies, I gradually came to the rather obvious conclusion that to prevent it ever happening again, I had to do something, anything, however small.

So, at the behest of a wonderful organisation called 'Courage to Care', I started giving modest presentations about my experiences and those of my fellow Hungarian Jews to schools and small community groups in Queensland, Australia – my tiny effort to keep the truth alive in the minds of generations that have no experience of war or lethal persecution.

Consequently, this memoir, or montage of memories as I like to put it, is merely, as one survivor poignantly said: 'a small piece in the stained-glass window depicting the horrors of the Holocaust'. I am not an academic, nor a historian; this story is simply my own truth. It is the story of a young infant girl caught up in war-torn Europe who, by the time she was six years old, had survived terror and trauma at the hands of both Nazis and Russians, before fleeing to Austria in 1948, the day before the communist regime came to arrest my father.

It is also the story of a woman who came to Australia as a young 'reffo' or refugee, and grew up in her new country conscious of, but not obsessive about, her perilous background; it is the story of a woman who, decades later, became increasingly compelled to find out more about her Jewish antecedents while deciding to teach new generations of the dangers of anti-Semitism and totalitarianism. These twin plagues still seem to walk the earth today – as I write, I'm witnessing the same sort of death and destruction being visited on Ukraine by yet another despot.

I was encouraged to undertake this literary journey by my friend Terence J. Quinn, a journalist and author; his remarkable research, writing and editing skills were invaluable. The result, my memoir, is dedicated to my beloved family, including my parents Les and Elizabeth, and grandparents Jeno and Irma, as well as the hundreds of thousands of their fellow Hungarian Jews who did not survive the *Shoah*.

Hamakom y'nachem etchem b'toch sh'ar availai tziyon ee yerushalayim. May God comfort you among all the mourners of Zion and Jerusalem.

Suzi Smeed

née Zsuzsannah Kalmar

Noosa / 2022

PART ONE
40 A.D. to 1943

"Some people like the Jews, and some do not. But no thoughtful man can deny the fact that they are, beyond any question, the most formidable and most remarkable race which has appeared in the world."

Sir Winston Churchill

CHAPTER 1

Jews: The scapegoats of history

THE ENTIRE history of Budapest has been inextricably intertwined with that of the Jews in Europe for nearly two thousand years. And what is both interesting and horrifying to learn is that the German Reich was not the first to oppress and repress the Jews in Hungary; it was not even the first regime to try to relocate or exterminate them.

Indeed, ever since the Romans first arrived north of the Danube in about 40AD, different monarchies, nation states and empires have pursued targeted and often violent policies of persecution and pogroms against my Jewish forebears.

There have been humans living beside or near the River Danube since Neolithic times. But the history of Budapest really only started a few decades after the death of Christ when a Roman cavalry unit attacked a small Celtic development on the east side of the river; the ruins of a former Roman garrison called Aquincum can be found in the northwest side of Budapest today (when I visited the city in 2002, we stayed at the Aquincum Hotel near the site). More than a hundred years later, Marcus Aurelius and his legions were still using the military base as a HQ for their northern campaigns.

The first recorded hint of a true Hungarian presence came in the late ninth century when a Magyar tribal chieftain took up residence in what had been the last Roman governor's palace. It took another century before King Stephen 1 established a Christian kingdom called Buda. Across the river a small Slavonic settlement called Pest already existed.

In the centuries that followed, Buda suffered the unwelcome attentions of first the Mongols, and then the Turks. The Holy Roman Emperor Leopold 1 laid siege to Buda in 1684 before liberating it from the Ottoman Empire. This was a grisly precursor to the Russian siege of Budapest two hundred and sixty years later.

Then it was the turn of the Austrian Habsburg monarchy to take control and in 1867 Buda and Pest both became part of the newly formed Austro-Hungarian Empire that lasted up until the First World War. In 1872, the two cities were united in a single municipality comprising ten districts.

Budapest was born.

The first Jews reportedly arrived in the area around the time of Emperor Marcus Aurelius when the Roman legions brought back prisoners or slaves to Aquincum from the wars in Judea and Syria. But by 400AD, the Roman Empire was in decline and the Huns and Goths had booted them out of the Danube region.

But not much is known about the 'Izraelita' community in Buda until 20 May 1092 when, in another chilling foretaste of what was to come during the second world war, a decree was issued by King Ladislaus 1 forbidding Jews to have Christian wives or slaves. Ladislaus's successor, King Coloman added further prohibitions relating to commerce and banking.

In the centuries since then, other monarchies and empires (and even Popes) have subjected Hungarian Jews to similar restrictions and repression. For example, at the Synod of Buda in 1279, it was decreed that every Jew should wear a distinguishing piece of red cloth on their upper garment in public. Sound familiar? Seven centuries later, the Nazis merely changed the colour to yellow.

Jews were also expelled from the country, not just once, but twice. First in 1349, during the Black Death, and then, after they'd been readmitted, again in 1360. Several years later, when Hungary was in financial straits, the Jews were asked to return but were slapped with heavy taxes for the privilege.

During the Ottoman era, they fared even worse. In 1526, Sultan Suleiman 1, after sacking Buda, ruled that the city's Hebrew community should be 'relocated' to other parts of his empire. Again, does that sound familiar?

And so, it goes on. In 1686, the Habsburg armies massacred many, if not most of the Jews in Buda. A female monarch, Queen Maria Theresa expelled the Jews from Buda yet again in 1746. And, in the mid-nineteenth century, there were pogroms against Hebrew communities in several provincial Hungarian cities.

Thereafter, it's only fair to say that there was a long period in Hungary when my Jewish ancestors prospered somewhat. Emancipation laws were enacted, providing more freedom from persecution, and winding back prohibitions relating to education, land ownership and commerce. Their religious, cultural and educational facilities began sprouting up across the country.

By the time my father was born in 1909, around nine hundred thousand Izraelita were well-integrated into mainstream Hungarian society; Budapest had a quarter of the country's Jews, making it the city with the third largest Jewish population in the world behind New York and Warsaw. In 1911, the mayor of Vienna sneeringly referred to Hungary's capital as 'Judapest'.

Most Jews at that time saw themselves as Hungarians; they might practise the Jewish faith, but Hungarian was their primary language. Many adopted Hungarian names. My father's family, for example, changed their surname from Kohn to Kalmár in 1913 before the Great War. Jews had also begun to achieve high positions in medicine, law and politics. The Hungarian government even had a smattering of Jewish ministers.

Happy times indeed for the Hungarian Jewry. A golden age even. Both sets of my grandparents were born during this period. They lived their early lives relatively free from the sort of persecution that had dogged their antecedents for generations. My maternal grandmother and grandfather could not have had any idea that, one day, they would end up in a place like Auschwitz.

It was not long before history began repeating itself yet again. The end of WW1 brought with it more angst and upheaval for the Jews despite the fact that thousands of them had fought for Hungary, including both my grandfathers, with many of them dying for their country. Hungary had been a part of the losing team and paid accordingly. The Austro-Hungarian empire was dissolved and much of its territory was ceded to neighbouring nations by the Allies.

The first post-war liberal Hungarian government was ousted by a communist-inspired mini-revolution; this so-called Hungarian Soviet Republic only lasted a few months before being quashed by Hungarian nationalist forces led by former admiral Miklos Horthy. Horthy, a former war hero, took power at the head of a conservative-nationalist coalition and would lead the country for the next twenty-five years and become a hugely controversial figure during the next world war.

Horthy once wrote: "I have been an anti-Semite throughout my life. I have never had contact with Jews. I have considered it intolerable that here in Hungary everything, every factory, bank, large fortune, business, theatre, press, commerce, etc. should be in Jewish hands, and that the Jew should be the image reflected of Hungary, especially abroad." His actions would have a catastrophic impact on the fortunes of the Jewish population, including my family.

In 1920, the Hungarian parliament ratified the 'Numerus Clausus' law that limited the number of Jews attending university. It is generally regarded as Europe's first such law of the twentieth century; but more such policies were ushered in during the interwar period as Horthy and other Hungarian leaders aligned themselves with the fascist governments of Germany and Italy.

Fast forward to 1938, the first of three more savage anti-Jewish decrees were announced, based on Germany's Nuremberg Laws; the first limited the number of Jews who could work in the law or medicine, or the government, or even commerce, to twenty percent. The following year that was reduced further to just five percent; two hundred and fifty thousand Hungarian Jews lost their jobs as a result.

In 1939, another decree saw Hungarian Jews defined racially for the first time; individuals with two or more Jewish grandparents were classed as Jewish. A third decree stipulated that a Jewish man who had non-marital sex with a 'decent non-Jewish woman resident in Hungary' could be sentenced to three years in prison.

As I write this, it is easy to get lost in the anonymous detail of these actions and events and their inexorable momentum towards the eventual annihilation of the 'Izraelita'; to become numb against the grief and the tragedy that affect so many individuals and families. I had to remind myself that my own family were living through these traumatic, fearful times; that their parents, siblings and friends were not simply statistics but real human beings who breathed and loved and worked hard to make the best of their lives under the sinister shadow of fascism.

Sometimes, I just shake my head. How did my mum and dad feel when they laid their heads on the pillow at night? What did they think when they switched on the wireless in the evening and heard what was happening to the world around them? When did they begin to realise with dread that their Jewish blood might lead them to an obscene fate? Later, when they could not go outside for fear of being identified as Jews and constantly listened out for the sound of heavy boots running up the stairway, how did they deal with that relentless stress?

Living a safe and pleasant life here in Australia, the Lucky Country, free from tyranny and oppression (Covid excepted) I can't help but marvel at the resilience and resourcefulness of my parents; between 1940 and 1945 they faced seemingly implacable odds to keep themselves, and me, safe from crushing hardship in a concentration camp and probable death.

Like many survivors, they did not talk much about it afterwards. Elie Wiesel, who won a Nobel Peace Prize, said this about his ordeal in Auschwitz: "He who went through it will not reveal it, not really, not entirely. Between his memory and its reflection there is a wall, and it cannot be pierced. The past belongs to the past and the survivor does not recognize himself in the words linking him to it.'"

Nowadays, I feel sad, and a little bit stupid, that I did not sit both my parents down when they were still alive and make them tell me everything about that catastrophic and defining period in their lives; also, I bitterly regret not pumping them for more details of my Hungarian roots – their respective family trees and the branches that grew from them.

Now, tragically, it's way too late.

CHAPTER 2

A gnarled family tree

WHEN I first embarked on this journey of remembrance, I knew that, sadly, I had few close relatives: no siblings, no aunts, and just one uncle – my father's elder brother, Ferenc – but he died in tragic circumstances while travelling to Australia after the 1956 Hungarian Revolution. His son Robert Kalmar, my cousin, grew up to be a surgeon living in Coffs Harbour, Australia, and I have caught up with him and his family on a handful of occasions over the years. There may be some, distant kin back in Hungary but, if so, we are blissfully unaware of each other.

My father's parents died long before I was born – his father soon after the First World War, while his mother suffered a massive stroke in 1925 when he was just sixteen. And I was only a baby when my mother's parents Jeno and Irma Halasz were transported to Auschwitz in 1944. There are photographs of them taken a year before standing with me, aged one, at a street corner near their home in Papa, the town where they lived, 120km west of Budapest; I have a subsequent picture of me taken at the exact same spot when I returned there six decades later.

Sadly, being so young at the time, I have no personal memory of Jeno and Irma, but I do remember my mother talking about how her father was a shortish man while her mother was a tall, stately lady with thick dark hair that she she'd wear in a plait coiled on top of her head like a crown. Mum's face used to take on a distant look as she told me a familiar story about Jeno and Irma: "They would stroll around the streets of Papa before the war and, let me tell you, your grandfather's' pride that he had won and married this handsome woman was obvious to everyone."

And, looking at the pictures now, I see Irma was indeed a striking lady while my grandfather wore glasses and always seemed to be smartly dressed; to me, he looks a little like Mikhail Gorbachev (minus the birthmark on his forehead). I'm sure he would not mind me saying that his daughter Erzsebet fortunately inherited her good looks from her mother's side!

At the time of his murder, Jeno was the manager of a health centre and chairman of a Jewish charitable association – Mor Wahrmann – that had one hundred and eighty members; an old Papa document I found during my research said that he had led the organisation 'with great care and zeal'. He had served in the Magyar army during the first world war, and this exempted him from the various anti-Jewish laws enacted by the Hungarian parliament between 1918 and the beginning of the second world war. But his military record would not be enough to save him from the gas chamber.

Jeno and Irma (nee Weisz) welcomed my mother into the world on Sunday, 8 February 1914, just a few months before Archduke Francis Ferdinand was assassinated in Sarajevo and the Great War erupted. She was their only child.

At that time, before the Germans arrived and changed everything, Papa was a quiet, prosperous market town with a multitude of historic buildings; indeed, the centre of the town is now heritage protected. The Jews had been a strong presence there since first settling in 1748 and their talent for business allied to a capacity for hard work over subsequent centuries helped Papa become a major regional trade hub, as well as a centre for learning and culture. It became known as the 'Athens of the Transdanubia'.

By 1944, the 2,500-strong Hebrew community represented about ten percent of the town's population. Most deemed themselves as both proud Hungarians and devout Jews, seeing no conflict in this. In the centuries that they had lived in the town, they'd fought for their country and followed their religion in reasonable harmony.

Like their friends and family and the Jewish shopkeepers and artisans of the town, my grandparents, Jeno and Irma, would have respected their Jewish culture and religious traditions including the Sabbath and the dietary laws of kashrut; they would have worshipped in the town's splendid synagogue that was built in 1844 (and semi-destroyed and completely defiled by the Nazis exactly one hundred years later).

My father Laszlo was born on Sunday, 28 March 1909, the year that Ernest Shackleton found the South Pole, and Louis Bleriot became the first man to cross the English Channel in an aircraft. His parents, Isaac and Barbara Kohn, were both thirty-two years old at the time and already had another son, Ferenc, aged six; they lived at 22 Mosety Street in Budapest. Isaac was a tailor and in 1913 they changed their surname to Kalmar, in a bid to sound more Hungarian. Interestingly but perhaps not surprisingly, Kalmar is synonymous with 'merchant' or 'trader' in Hungarian. Dad was also lived up to his surname: he owned two textile shops in the city, one on Vilmos Csaszar Street (later renamed Bajcsy-Zsilinskzy Street by the Russians), the other on Anker Street, not far from our apartment.

In later life a staunch supporter of Israel, dad used to delight in telling people that the city of Ahuzat Bayit, later to become Tel Aviv, was founded by the Jewish community on the outskirts of Jaffa right about the same time as he arrived in the world. Nowadays, of course, it's a bustling metropolis of nearly half-a-million souls and the economic and technological heart of Israel.

Dad was thrilled when he visited it a few years before he died. I've also been there a couple of times and found it a wonderful, vibrant city, a cultural and culinary powerhouse on the edge of the Mediterranean. I was particularly struck to learn that the surrounding hills had been covered in trees before the Romans arrived in Judea in 73AD. The invaders then killed the trees with salt, presumably to prevent Jewish rebels from hiding there. In recent decades, however, the Israelis have replanted and many of those same hills are once again covered in beautiful trees. My mother would have loved the spectacle but sadly she never got to visit Israel. Instead, I planted a little tree there in her memory. A special moment.

Laszlo and Erzsebet were married in Budapest on 24 November 1940. A few days earlier, Hungary had signed the Berlin Pact, which was the agreement between the Axis powers of Germany, Italy and Japan; ominously, a few days later the Nazi propaganda film *The Eternal Jew* premiered in Berlin. Needless to say, it wasn't very sympathetic to the Hebrew race. On November 29, Hitler and his cronies issued their draft plan for *Operation Barbarossa* – the invasion of Russia. This would lead to their staggering defeat a few years later and the beginning of the end for the Third Reich. Crucially, for my family and my fellow Jews, this false and foolish step would also lead to the liberation of Hungary by the Red Army.

But, by then, it was too late for more than half a million Hungarian Jews.

CHAPTER 3

Courtship amidst chaos

MY PARENTS met for the first time in 1939 as the storm clouds were gathering in Europe; dad visited the young Erzsebet Halasz's office in Papa while there on business, and family legend has it that he took one look at the beautiful woman and announced that she would be his wife. My mother, however, was not impressed: "Do you think I'm some country hick you can take advantage of?" she famously replied.

My father was already divorced but had remained friends with his first wife, Livly Lukacz, whom he'd married a few years earlier when he was just 27 in Szekesfeharvar, a city situated halfway between Budapest and Papa. Lily would later die in the Holocaust.

At that time, dad was a young man about town; he enjoyed meeting new people and loved talking to friends and strangers alike in the Budapest's coffee houses and bars. In particular, he had two journalist friends. One was George Mikes who was then a young journalist working for the Budapest daily newspaper *Reggel* before moving to London in 1938 where he worked for the BBC's Hungarian Service, broadcasting back to his home country during the war. He went on to become a well-known humourist and writer, producing more than forty books.

Dad used to tell this story about the other journalist friend: "One day we were having a coffee and I noticed that the front of his shirt was covered in ink. A fountain pen had leaked from the breast pocket. I drew his attention to it, and he said that he was working on a solution to leaky pens." The man's name, dad would say at the end of his anecdote to dramatic effect, was ... Laszlo Biro. Biro, a Jew who would flee from the Nazis to South America with his brother George in 1943, went on to make a mint from his eponymous, and famous, ballpoint pen invention.

In the 1930s, Budapest was regarded as the 'The Paris of the East' and had a reputation as an exciting, exotic city situated squarely at the crossroads between East and West. The beautiful, sophisticated metropolis with its classical architecture, impressive monuments and verdant squares, boasted wonderful restaurants and coffee houses, as well as theatres and art galleries, many of them run by Jews.

In the years after we fled to Australia in 1948, I remember my parents reminiscing about how elegant and beautiful Budapest had been before the war reduced it to rubble and ruin. And I can just picture them stepping out together as a freshly minted couple in the months before hostilities broke out on 1 September 1939, when Germany invaded Poland. Where would they have gone around town when they were courting, I wonder?

Would, for example, my mother, then a lively, stylish twenty-five-year-old, have dragged my dad shopping on the magnificent 2.3km long Andrassy Avenue? The young couple might have taken a tram or just wandered arm-in-arm up the avenue from Erzsebet Square, past the Hungarian State Opera House towards Heroes Square and the vast Varosliget Park close to where my mother was living before their marriage – 108 Arena Street. It was close to the Royal Hungarian Army barracks.

Before the Nazis polluted it with their malign presence, Andrassy was the jewel in Budapest's cultural crown with its high-end boutiques and department stores and its theatres and embassies. When I visited the city in 2002, one of the most famous buildings in Budapest, 60 Andrassy Avenue – home sequentially to the Gestapo, the Arrow Cross fascists and the Soviet secret police – had just been made into a museum devoted to the beatings, torture and murder that had taken place within its cold, stone walls. The museum is, appropriately, called *Terrorhaza* – The House of Terror.

Strolling up this grand, tree-lined boulevard, the young lovestruck couple would have passed an endless stream of elegant women in fur-collared coats, knitted dresses or tailored suits, sporting high-crowned fedoras, cheerful cloches or slouchy hats worn at a jaunty angle and festooned with ribbons, feathers and bows, and strapped heels or tongued Oxfords. Their male companions might be smartly turned out in dark suits with padded shoulders and high-waisted, wide-fitting, cuffed trousers, or tweed sportscoats with homburgs or trilbies worn at a rakish angle. The more dashing among them might have been wearing two-toned brogues.

I can imagine mum and dad fitting in well with the city's smart set, particularly my mother. She liked to dress well, and with the family business being textiles, she had access to the best cloth for her clothes, many of which were hand tailored. She was a very attractive woman with light brown hair, a trim figure and a ready smile; her hair was often woven into an elegant plait on the top of her head, like her own mother's.

It is easy to remember her soft brown eyes crinkling as she laughed. At five-foot six, or 168cms, she was quite tall for the period. My dad, on the other hand, was only a few centimetres taller with wavy reddish-brown hair and green eyes (both of which I inherited). He wore glasses and had deep dimples when he smiled. Like my grandfather Jeno, he might have thought he was punching above his weight, but he was a confident, feisty character and no doubt swept my mum off her feet.

When they returned to Laszlo's apartment near Erzsebet Square, they might have treated themselves to hot chocolates to Fisherman's Bastion and many more including the five famous bridges that then spanned the river, including the Szechenyi Chain Bridge.

Both my parents loved music; my mum delighted in playing Hungarian folk songs on the piano, while dad used to take the score with him to the opera house and 'conduct the orchestra' from his seat! They both also liked movies and during their courting days, would go to one of Budapest's many picture palaces like the Forum Cinema (now the Pushkin Art Cinema) or the Royal Apollo which replaced the ballroom in the majestic Grand Hotel Royal (now the Corinthia) in Erzsebet Boulevard which, a few years later, would become a hideout for the Gestapo.

The Royal Apollo was a short walk from Andrassy Avenue. And maybe after a light supper of halaszle, a fish soup, or lecso, made with hot paprika, tomato, and sausage, washed down by palinka – a fruit brandy, the courting couple might have decided to watch a late-evening screening of a Hollywood musical such as the 'Wizard of Oz' which was a major hit in 1939, or perhaps a home-grown Hungarian film.

Ironically, the film makers in Budapest at the time were mostly Jewish professionals who had learnt their trade in the UK or the US. In the decades since the Royal Apollo had first opened in 1915, the Hungarian film community had spawned such luminaries as director Michael Korda (born Sandor Laszlo Kellner), and famous actors Peter Lorre (born Laszlo Lowenstein) and Béla Lugosi (born Bela Blasko).

Now, as I look back to that brief tranquil time in Budapest before the Holocaust, I take some comfort in the fact that my parents at least had that opportunity to get to know each other and come to the wonderful conclusion that they were meant to be together for all time. In 1939, as the looming war cast shadows over their burgeoning love and frail optimism, it would have been a bittersweet time. The calm before the storm.

As they snuggled close together and sipped their drinks in the Café Gerbaud, Laszlo and Erzsebet could not have remotely dreamt what evil lurked in the shadows and how fraught their lives would become before too long.

CHAPTER 4

War and a wedding

MY FATHER was an avid reader his whole life, and largely self-educated; he was also passionate about politics and current affairs. When Germany invaded Poland in September 1939, I can just see him poring over the newspapers and listening to the wireless, eager for news of how the war was progressing in Europe.

Did he have any inkling then as to how bad things would get for the Jews? For him and his loved ones? Unlikely. No one could have dreamt at that early stage that the Reich would set about exterminating millions of people in death camps

And, as a patriotic Hungarian, did he welcome the news in November 1940 that Regent Miklos Horthy had committed Hungary to join the unholy Axis alliance of Germany, Italy and Japan? Again unlikely; like many Hungarians at the time, dad was an Anglophile, and it is more likely that he was horrified by Horthy's Faustian pact with Hitler.

What is certain is that, just four days after Hungary became an Axis member, Laszlo Kalmar put aside any thoughts and feelings he had about the perilous world events and married his sweetheart Erzsebet Halasz on Sunday, 24 November 1940, in a civil ceremony in Budapest.

My favourite photograph of my parents shows them on that day, arm in arm, beautifully dressed – she in a white dress with a floral pattern and he in a suit and tie; she's clutching a bouquet of flowers, one hand holds a homburg, the other is in his jacket pocket. They are standing proudly in a garden area, both sporting radiant smiles. These days, I look at it often, mostly with bittersweet thoughts – delight in their young, unaffected happiness and love for each other, and hopes for the future, and despair over the imminent horror that would soon face, replacing those smiles progressively with gloom, with fear and then with unmitigated terror.

In a cruel irony, around the same time my parents were getting married in November 1940, the Warsaw Ghetto was sealed off by the Nazis, effectively incarcerating 380,000 Polish Jews in a designated area enclosed by a ten-foot-high wall topped by barbed wire and closely guarded by German troops. Their actions in Warsaw set the pattern for what would later happen in Hungary: just days after the Germans entered Warsaw, they ordered the establishment of a Jewish Council to help with the implementation of the Reich's orders, and to administer the ghetto – just as they did in Budapest a few years later.

In Warsaw, the template for the Nazi's execution of the Endlosung throughout Europe was formulated, although the full horror of the Final Solution itself was not itself formalised until early 1942; this happened at the Wannsee Conference in Berlin when Reinhard Heydrich, Heinrich Himmler's deputy, chaired a meeting of fifteen senior officials of the Nazi party and the German government, all men, at a lakeside villa in the fashionable Berlin suburb where wealthy Germans had their homes.

SS Lieutenant Colonel Adolf Eichmann, who would go on to play a diabolical role in the Hungarian Holocaust, organised the infamous event as if it was a routine business meeting – a normal day's work for busy executives. A female stenographer sat in the background taking the minutes. What was that woman thinking, I wonder, as she scribbled her shorthand notes? Did her pencil wobble at all during the gory details? How did she sit calmly during all that clinical talk about murdering innocent people on an industrial scale? Did her husband ask her when she got home that evening – "How was your day, liebling?" To which she might have replied – "Oh, just the usual, dear. The chaps were just nutting out a strategy to annihilate millions of those problematic Jewish people." Did she go on to live an ordinary life after the war?

It is astonishing to realise that it took the Wannsee participants just *ninety minutes* to map out calmly and clinically, the plans and logistics for what would result in the annihilation of more than six million Jews. The banality of evil, indeed.

None of this heinous, genocidal plotting on the part of the Nazis would have been known to my mum and dad, of course, as they stood together on that cold Sunday in the Budapest Registry Office on their wedding day; they were both happy and nervous as they committed to love each other for better or worse, for richer or poorer, in sickness and health, and to love and cherish each other from that day forward until death did part them. I can picture my mother in her pretty dress, clutching a small bouquet, her young, sweet face and warm, radiant smile as she turned to kiss her new husband – both mercifully oblivious to the calamitous events that would soon befall their small family.

I was born twenty-two months later on 12 September 1942. While my mum was pregnant with me, she told everyone that she wanted a pretty little girl called Suzi with red curly hair and a pretty smile. According to my dad, however, Zsuzsanna Borbala Kalmar arrived in this world a skinny little wretch with blotchy skin and scraggy dark hair. "I'm going to have to work hard to marry her off," he joked when he first saw me.

I only possess a Xeroxed copy of my birth certificate; it was issued in Budapest in 1964, almost exactly twenty-two years after I was born in war-torn Europe. Presumably the original was lost sometime during our various attempts to escape the Nazis and the

Russians. The certified copy does not include much in the way of details other than the names of my parents, the date and the fact that I was a girl; there is no weight recorded, and no specific time or place of birth other than 'Budapest'.

My mother once told me that I was born in our roomy apartment in Deak Ferenc Street, next to Erzsebet Square and a few blocks from St Stephen's Basilica. I do know that she had the help of a nanny and a maid (a mother and daughter, both of whom were Christians), as was common at the time for middle class families.

But, while I was greedily drinking my mother's milk, the war continued unabated. Just a week before my arrival, Russian planes dropped seventeen heavy bombs on Budapest, presumably in retaliation for the enthusiastic participation of Hungarian troops in Operation Barbarossa – the German invasion of the Soviet Union. Two months earlier, in July 1942, the Nazis had started systematically gassing Jews at their new Auschwitz camp, and more than a quarter million Jews had been transported from the Warsaw Ghetto to another killing centre at Treblinka.

And, in the interval between their wedding day and my birth, the Japanese attacked Pearl Harbour, the German army ran rampant in Russia, Britain declared war on Hungary, and Singapore fell to the Japanese. Meanwhile, French Jews were ordered to wear the yellow Star of David. But by late 1942, the Axis powers were in the ascendant. The only otherwise bright spot during that time was that Reinhardt Heydrich, the brute who chaired the Wannsee Conference, was fatally wounded in Prague by Czech soldiers.

Ironically, the Jews in Hungary still felt comparatively safe at that point. While millions of their fellow Israelites in other European countries had already been brutalised, deported and murdered, Horthy's alliance with the Axis powers had thus far prevented the Nazis from implementing their heinous Final Solution in Hungary.

The majority of the country's Jewry, while apprehensive about the increasing atmosphere of anti-Semitism, and perhaps hit hard socially and economically by losing their jobs and/or their homes as a result of the punitive Jewish decrees, did not feel their lives were in actual danger at that point.

With the addition of a new baby to feed and protect, it's quite probable that, by then, my father was growing increasingly anxious about the way things were going in the world. It is highly probable that he would have heard in late-night wireless broadcasts about the escalation of the Nazis' annihilation of Jews throughout Europe.

There has been a lot of debate about how aware Jews in Hungary actually were about what unspeakable atrocities were happening to their counterparts in other European countries. According to authoritative reports I've read, as many as forty percent of Hungarian citizens listened to foreign news broadcasts during the war – American, British or Soviet radio stations – which indicates that details of the Final Solution might have reached a wide audience before the Germans occupied Hungary in 1944.

After the war, many Jews claimed they knew little or nothing about the death camps until they themselves, their friends and families were rounded up in ghettoes before being transported to Auschwitz. Yet the BBC had first aired information about Holocaust atrocities in June 1942. Subsequent radio reports from the Voice of America and *Kossuth Radio*, the Hungarian language radio channel sponsored by Moscow, also reported on the Third Reich's savage persecution of the Jews in Europe.

I'm certain my father would have greedily distilled and dissected every snippet of information gleaned from the BBC or other sources. And that would explain why he and my mother decided to convert to Catholicism in October 1943 at the church of Krisztina Varos (known as Our Lady of the Snows) on the Buda side of the river.

Knowing dad, this was not for religious reasons; it would

have been purely a tactical move on his part, hoping against hope that by renouncing their Hebrew faith, his little family might be better protected against the looming threat. This was an echo of his father Isaak's decision in 1913 to change the family name from Kohn to the more Hungarian-sounding Kalmar in order to become more assimilated.

So, he would have been totally stunned when, less than six months later, the whole world turned upside down.

and pastries at the Cafe Gerbeaud in Vorosmarty Square which opened in 1858 with Louis XIV rococo furnishings, gold chandeliers and tinkling piano music. It was just one of the capital's many coffee houses and tea rooms in the pre-war years patronised by the city's intellectuals, artists and sophisticates. It's still there today and more or less intact.

As Laszlo and Erzsebet cheerfully sipped their drinks, did my father read out some stories from that day's *Nepszava* (People's Voice) newspaper, or perhaps the *Magyar Nemzet* (Hungarian Nation) to his gorgeous new girlfriend? God knows, with what was happening in Europe at the time, there would have been no shortage of shock, horror to read and talk about.

On reflection, it's more likely he would have tried to keep mum's spirits up by relating some gossip about Budapest's glamorous Gabor sisters – Zsa Zsa, Magda and Eva. Zsa Zsa had been crowned Miss Hungary in 1936 before starting her acting career. She and her siblings would emigrate to the US before the Nazi occupation, probably anticipating that the Jewish ancestry of both their parents might cause them some grief.

Perhaps one weekend the young lovers might have 'taken the waters', following in the footsteps of millions of locals since Roman times who revitalized their bodies, minds and spirits by visiting one of the city's famous medicinal spas. Budapest lies across a network of more than one hundred and twenty-five thermal springs. For example, they could have gone to the Szechenyi thermal baths at City Park, a vast water complex of pools, saunas, steam cabins and massage rooms, or the Kiraly Baths that were originally built by the Turks in 1565.

Or the pair could have taken a lazy Sunday afternoon cruise along the Danube, the young businessman proudly pointing out to the girl from the small town of Papa all the capital's scenic splendours: from the thirteenth century Buda Castle and the Liberty Statue to the medieval church ruins on Margaret Island,

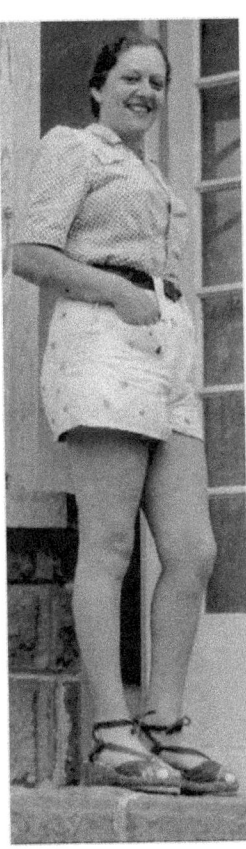

Above: My beloved mother Erzsebet as a young woman in Papa before the war.

Top right: Mum with her parents Jeno and Irma Halasz who were murdered in Auschwitz. Both my mother and I were supposed to be with them on that fateful journey, but we escaped only days before the transportation.

Bottom right: The brass memorial plaque I placed at the Mt Gravatt Holocaust Shrine.

Mum & Dad on their wedding day, 24 November 1940. How happy and relaxed they look, totally oblivious to the unspeakable terror that would lie ahead.

Top: My birth certificate. 12 September 1942, Budapest.

Above: My parents' wedding certificate. 24 November 1940 in Budapest. If you look closely, you can see Samu Stern's name as a witness in the column second from the right.

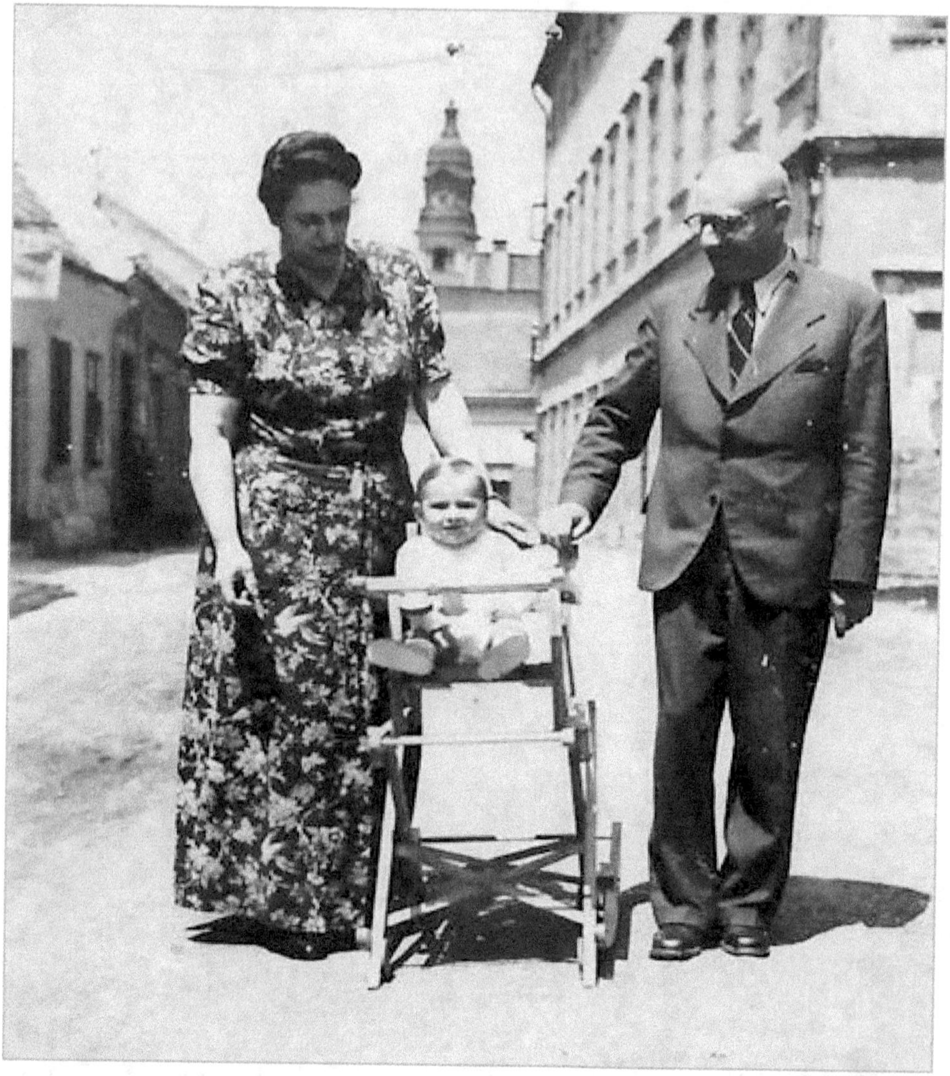

Above: My grandparents Jeno and Irma with me outside their house in Papa 1943. A year later they would be murdered in Auschwitz.

Right: Nearly sixty years later, I stand in exactly the same spot on a return visit to Hungary with John. The steeple of the Catholic church can be seen in the background of both photos.

As I have dared to 'bare all' in this memoir, it is perhaps appropriate that two out of the only three photos that I have of my childhood in Hungary picture me without any clothes on! I believe these were taken in in the summer of 1945, not long after the war ended.

Three years, three countries ...

Top left: Happily posing with flowers in 1947 at Lake Baloton near Budapest, my parents' favourite holiday place.

Above left: Newly arrived in Austria 1948 after our daring escape.

Right: Safe at last in Australia.

PART TWO

1944 –1945

"I cannot exaggerate the brutality of the Germans in Hungary. What the Germans are doing is nothing less than setting up abattoirs in Europe into which are shepherded thousands of Jews. They are despatched with the sort of brutal efficiency in which the Prussians delight. This is the biggest scandal in the history of human crime."

Brendan Bracken, Great Britain's Minister of Information (1944)

CHAPTER 5

The hounds of hell

ON 19 March 1944, Adolf Hitler gave the green light to *Operation Margarethe*: eleven *Wehrmacht* divisions, mobilised from military bases in Austria, swept through the western regions of Hungary to Budapest like a warm knife through butter.

Led by SS-Obergruppenführer (lieutenant general) Otto Winkelmann, the occupying forces met little or no resistance on the way. Suddenly, almost without warning, the Hungarian capital's streets were full of noisy military motorcycles and vehicles manned by sinister SS soldiers toting machine-guns. German patrols took up their positions; some occupied the radio stations and transmitters, others guarded the railway stations, while the Hungarian ministries and army offices were all surrounded by SS tanks.

Key downtown buildings were draped in giant swastika flags and banners. Planeloads of SS troopers arrived at airfields throughout Hungary. The Sicherheitsdienst or SD (Security Services) and the Gestapo requisitioned the Astoria Hotel for their use and seized control of all police activities in Budapest.

By midday the country had been entirely taken over.

The Nazi occupation of Hungary would last less than a year, but it was to have horrific lifetime consequences for the country and in particular the Jewish population.

Hitler had reacted with rage when he learnt that their Axis partner Hungary was making secret overtures to the Allies in the aftermath of the failed invasion of the Soviet Union; he had invited the Hungarian Regent Miklos Horthy to Salzburg on 15 March, ostensibly for cordial talks, but this was just a ruse; four days later, when Horthy arrived back in Budapest, he was shocked to find Nazi soldiers waiting to greet him at the railway station and German guards outside the Palace. The Regent was then placed under house arrest where he continued nominally to rule the country while under German duress.

The Reich's plenipotentiary in Hungary, Edmund Veesenmayer, a Nazi zealot who regarded Jews as the 'number one enemy', forced the Regent to appoint a new right-wing, pro-German government under the leadership of Dome Sztojay – a former ambassador to Berlin, and a noted anti-Semite.

On 22 March, the new Sztojay cabinet immediately set about mobilizing the whole Magyar machinery of public servants, gendarmes and policemen to make the country *Judenfrei*. By the time when, four months later, Sztojay stepped down due to ill health in July 1944, almost the entire Jewish population outside Budapest had been expunged from Hungarian soil. In 1945, this odious man – described as a 'Magyar Quisling' – was found guilty of war crimes by a Hungarian court and sentenced to death by firing squad.

On the first day of the occupation, a high-level Nazi arrived in Budapest with a diabolical plan. Adolf Eichmann, a former travelling salesman, but now a murderer of Jews on an industrial scale, immediately set to work on the 'Ungarnaktion' – the deportation and subsequent extermination of the Hungarian Jewry. Aided and abetted by Sztojay's Minister of the Interior, Andor Jaross and his two rabidly anti-Semitic state secretaries, Laszlo Endre and Laszlo Baky, the relative shielding of Hungary's Jewry from the worst excesses of the Holocaust came to an abrupt and appalling end.

Thanks to his bloody experience in other European countries, Eichmann had acquired all the dark skills and strategies required to complete this last piece of the Final Solution. He had a well-worked strategy: this included threats and promises to Jewish leaders, and alternating intimidation and reassurance. Eichmann knew that, despite only having a relatively small SS Judenkommando at his disposal – estimates range from 120 to 200 men – he would be able to rely on the enthusiastic and energetic support of the Hungarian authorities, police and gendarmerie to expedite his plans. Sadly, he was right.

On their second day in town, Eichmann's SS henchmen visited the main offices of the Pest Jewish community at 12 Sip Street and announced that an eight-member Judenrat – Central Jewish Council – was to be formed; its first job would be to prepare reports on the structure, property and key people involved in the Jewish community. They emphasised that there were to be no disruptions in the usual order of religious services and that the rabbis should reassure their congregations.

This council was to be presided over by the reluctant but resigned Samuel Stern, who was my mother's 'bacsi' and had been a witness at my parents' wedding in 1940. Stern was then seventy years old and had already been leader of the city's main Jewish congregation for fifteen years.

Eichmann knew that a such a group would be vital in helping to sugar-coat the bitter pills that he would soon be dispensing to the country's Jews. He needed them to keep calm, to follow orders and not cause disruption while he set about his diabolical schemes. Similar but smaller councils were set up in regional areas across Hungary, including my mother's hometown of Papa, with the same *raison d'etre*. These, however, did not last long – usually only a matter of weeks – because the Nazi killing machine would soon render them unnecessary.

In less than a week, a blizzard of regulations were gazetted in the papers and posted on the walls of buildings: Jews must not leave their home between the hours of 7pm and 7am, must not travel in cars, must travel in the rear of trams, must not go further than five kilometres from their home, must not shop at times other than between 3pm and 4 pm; all cameras and radios owned by Jews had to be delivered to the nearest police station. All jewellery, gold or silver and all pocket and wrist watches owned by Jews had to be delivered to the nearest bank.

Like all Jews in Hungary at that perilous moment in history, my parents had been shocked by the speed and efficiency of the German occupation. And yet I know my father would not have panicked; instead, his scheming mind would have immediately begun computing strategies to survive this new catastrophe.

But even he could not have foreseen the two events that would soon change all our lives.

CHAPTER 6

Forced into Nazi slavery

AT THE beginning of April 1944, dad was suddenly and forcibly taken away from his life, his business and his family to be conscripted into a Hungarian slave labour battalion.

The Labour Service System, Kotelezo Munkaszolgálat, under the control of the Hungarian Ministry of Defence, had initially included men deemed to be 'unreliable' and 'unworthy to carry weapons'; these were sundry socialists, communists, gypsies and other dissident enemies, real or perceived, of the right-wing regime. Homosexuals too.

By 1944, there were around sixty purely Jewish labour companies numbering many tens of thousands of men wearing yellow stars and yellow armbands who had been set to work in mines, on rail projects and military construction projects; at least forty thousand of them had already been sent to the Eastern front to serve alongside the Second Hungarian Army.

There they endured appalling conditions and a daily diet of hunger, harassment and humiliation as well as extreme danger: often the Jews would be sent in advance to march across a suspected minefield to trigger any devices. Only about a quarter of the nearly fifty thousand who had been sent to the Eastern front survived.

My father, by comparison, was lucky: he was assigned to a labour company that was upgrading the Rakoczifalva airfield at Szolnok, about one hundred kilometres east of Budapest. Between 1943-44, the Hungarian air force had a sizeable base there with nearly seven hundred men, including thirty-four officers, while the Luftwaffe was reported to have had twelve hundred pilots and crew. The planes included Messerschmidt ME 110s, Stuka dive bombers and Focke-Wulf light bombers.

Dad and his fellow munkaszolgat, Jewish slave labourers, were ordered to level and extend the runway area. The work itself was hard, but not backbreaking. But they were poorly dressed and badly fed – ersatz coffee made from chicory, stale, hard black bread, and meat on rare occasions. The biggest problem was health and sanitation. Living in crowded wooden barracks, they suffered constantly from diarrhoea, and flea and lice infestations. Typhoid was common.

Dad once told me that he would go to a river near the labour camp and wash himself with the ice so he wouldn't get lice. Ironically, much later, when the war ended, he went to a barber shop and sat in a chair just vacated by a Russian soldier; he later found lice on his neck and, as a result, he came down with typhus and was very sick for a while. Family legend has it that, when he recovered, he ate twelve cream cheese pancakes in one sitting!

My father was a sturdy, scrappy bloke who kept himself fit his whole life – doing push-ups in his eighties – so he was able to cope. He was always the kind to make the best of any situation, however bad; he certainly wasn't going to let a few filthy fascists do him down.

To begin with he kept his head down and out of trouble. He even told me many years later that the German crewmen had mostly dealt with the Jewish prisoners in what he described as a 'gentlemanly way', unlike their more vicious Hungarian overseers who treated their Jewish work slaves like dogs. But all that changed when the Gestapo arrived one day; things took a sinister turn and my father inevitably got himself into trouble.

At the airfield, he and his workmates had been split into three working units and were told that whichever unit worked the hardest during the week would be allowed weekend leave. Dad, ever the pragmatist, suggested to his colleagues that the units simply take turns to work the hardest and that way they'd all get to see their families over time.

Unfortunately, one of the other guys dobbed him in as the ringleader of the scheme and the Gestapo decided to teach him a lesson. He was beaten, tied up with a piece of wood behind his knees and left outside in the cold and rain for twenty-four hours. I can't think what went on his mind during that terrible night, but I bet he wondered if he'd ever see his wife and daughter again.

Years later, during the sixties, when we were safe in Sydney, we received word that the then German government had announced that it would pay reparations to people who'd been forced into the Labour Service during the war. We urged dad to apply and, reluctantly, he did, only to receive a letter soon after saying: 'We regret we cannot pay you any compensation because, according to our records you were guilty of sabotage while you were working for the service.' So typical of dad!

Fortunately, he survived his cruel punishment at Rakoczifalva but worse was to follow. Shortly after this incident, in July 1944, my mother was alerted by her 'uncle' Samu Stern that her husband's work unit was about to be sent to the Russian Front – a virtual death sentence. In the event, only two hundred of the two thousand men in his work group came home after the war.

When my mother sent a frantic message to her husband warning him of what was about to happen, once again my father's quick thinking and pragmatism came into play; he quickly feigned appendicitis and was sent to a field hospital while his mates were being shipped out to the bloody battlefields of Russia. However, in the process of having his perfectly healthy appendix taken out, he had a bad reaction to ether, contracted pneumonia and took a long time to recover. At least he escaped with his life – forty-thousand other Jews in the forced labour service were not so lucky.

Knowing dad, the day after his bogus operation he would have lain back in his field hospital bed with a satisfied smile on his lips, congratulating himself on his ingenuity but oblivious to the peril his wife and daughter were now in.

CHAPTER 7

The gates of hell

MY FATHER would have fallen out of that same hospital bed if he had known that we were at that same moment incarcerated in a crowded, disease-ridden ghetto waiting to be transported to Auschwitz and certain death.

As the saying goes, "The road to hell is paved with good intentions." With dad gone, my mother had decided to take me to Papa to see her parents. Her intention: to persuade them to return with us to Budapest and hide from the Nazis. It is fair to say that things did not work out quite as she had hoped.

When we arrived in her birthplace at the end of April 1944, things had already deteriorated for the town's Jews. For a start, they were wearing the yellow Star of David patch – the 'mediaeval sign of mockery' – as one historian described it, as they walked up and down the familiar cobbled streets with slouched shoulders and worried expressions. The humiliating yellow 'Judenstern' had been mandated across Hungary from April 5, and those marked by it faced daily harassment from both the gendarmerie and non-Jewish residents alike. This regularly took the form of violence, with innocent Jews being verbally abused and physically assaulted in the street.

In Papa, the Nazis had already appointed a five-member Judenrat to do their cruel bidding. Jews were forbidden to use public transportation. All radios were confiscated, preventing us from receiving any news. Possession of typewriters and bicycles were forbidden as well. Suddenly, there were German forces all over the town and in the streets, determined to confiscate the wealth of the 'Izraelita'. Jewish businesses were seized along with all cash and jewellery. The Nazi officers were housed in the most desirable Jewish homes. Increasing regulations spelled increased shortages. Suddenly there was no meat and fresh produce was hard to get.

Along with the seizure of the homes and furniture, the appropriation of all personal property soon followed. According to the new regulations published by the fascists in the official county newspapers: 'The Jews are obliged to immediately surrender all personal cash, silverware, carpets, art. They are notified that all real property must be immediately listed with the county notary. Sale or transfer of any such property is strictly forbidden on pain of punishment.'

Then, in the last week of May, came the SS order for the creation of a ghetto. It followed a Hungarian government statement: 'The Royal Hungarian government is preparing to cleanse the nation from Jews. This cleansing will be conducted region by region, regardless of age or gender, and all Jews are therefore to be shipped to the designated concentration areas. The deportation will be conducted by area police and gendarme forces.'

The small area designated for the Papa ghetto was in the town centre where most Jews lived; it was located in and around a tight grid of four streets that ran roughly parallel east to west: Szent Laszlo, Petofi, Eotvos and Rakoczi, and bounded on the west side by Bastya Street and Kossuth Street on the east side. The new ghetto was about a half-kilometre square, containing small houses and apartments, anchored by the large synagogue that was the pride and joy of the town's Jewish community. Later, Hungarian fascists would defile the temple by using it as stable for their horses, smashing the prized stained-glass windows and desecrating the Torah scrolls that remained.

Over two days, 24 and 25 May, every Jewish man, woman

and child in Papa, along with roughly three hundred from the surrounding towns and villages (including Nemesszlok where Samuel Stern was born) were rounded up and forced to move into the ghetto – a total of more than 2,500. There were two gates at either end of the ghetto and Jews had to enter through one of them carrying whatever scant possessions they were allowed to carry. Even then, the black-clad SS troopers and the Hungarian gendarmes in their distinctive cock-feathered caps checked their meagre bundles for money or jewellery; sometimes, at random, their only change of underwear was also confiscated.

Unknown to the citizens of Papa, similar actions were taking place right across provincial Hungary during May 1944, with ghettoes being set up in scores of cities, towns and villages outside the capital Budapest.

My grandparents' house was just a block away from the Papa ghetto, in Kozep Street. My mother remembered carrying me in her arms as she and her parents slowly walked the hundred metres or so to the ghetto gate at Rakoczi Street near Kossuth Street, amid the cries of frightened children and the screams of innocent Jews being humiliated and beaten by the police.

"It was," she told me once, "like going through the gates of Hell." Meanwhile, non-Jewish residents stood in the street and watched, many of them openly showing their contempt. At last, their faces seemed to say, the Jews are getting their come-uppance ... and now it's time for us to get our hands on their loot.

Conditions inside the closed-in ghetto were appalling. Two-and-a-half thousand people crammed into four blocks like sardines, their world turned upside down and the future a vast, scary unknown. Supplies were scarce and sanitary conditions shocking. The commander in charge of supervising the ghetto was a local civil servant, Pal Lotz. After the war, this hated figure escaped to Switzerland where he became a hotel manager. Ironically, when he discovered that he was a wanted person for his crimes, Lotz then fled to Australia and, using a pseudonym, disappeared from sight. Sadly, he never paid for his crimes.

I think about my mother, heavy of heart, trudging slowly and sadly to the ghetto with me in her arms. What was she feeling as the gates closed behind her? Did she curse her decision to go to Papa? Did she think she might never see her husband again? How could she protect her child? These are questions I wished I'd asked her before she died prematurely aged just sixty-six.

I also think about grandma and grandpa Irma and Jeno who would have left the house they had lived in for much of their married life, their furniture, photos and mementoes the only remaining testament to their lives. In their hearts, did they know that they would never see their home, or their possessions, ever again? That the Nazis and their Hungarian collaborators would exterminate them?

Both of my grandparents' names were featured on the 'List of Martyrs' which was part of an exhibition called 'Our Forgotten Neighbours' shown in the ruins of the Papa synagogue in 2012 to commemorate Papa's vibrant pre-war Jewish community. It memorialises the ninety-per cent of the town's Jews who died during the Holocaust, mostly in the death camps. Of the 2,565 deportees, only three hundred made it back. The number of murdered children totalled 671.

For their descendants like me, in the absence of a grave and tombstone, it will have to do. Although, more recently, I organised a brass memorial plaque for Jeno and Irma at the Holocaust shrine at the Mt Gravatt Jewish Cemetery. It gave me a certain peace of mind.

CHAPTER 8

Deportation Zone V

MY MOTHER was always a practical, pragmatic woman; she had a sensitive side too, but I don't doubt she would have faced up with fortitude and grace to the horrors of sharing a confined space with more than two thousand others crammed in beside her in the ghetto.

Nonetheless, she had a baby and her ageing parents to consider besides herself. And remember, she was just thirty years old at the time. But I'm guessing that she would have done her best to the make the best of the 'new normal' that she found herself enduring in the ghetto, not least having to share a room with several other strangers.

Life in the wartime Jewish ghettoes has been (rightly) well documented in the decades since the Shoah ... a vast, collective chronicle of starvation, disease and abuse. I don't remember anything about the weeks spent in the Papa ghetto so I cannot add anything to the record from my personal experience. But it is not hard to imagine how difficult and harrowing it must have been, particularly for mothers of young children. The fear, the uncertainty, the bewilderment that their lives could be arbitrarily destroyed in this way.

In the five weeks that the Papa ghetto existed, only a few people were allowed in and out. These included men and women who were deemed fit to work as forced agricultural labourers in the surrounding fields, plus a few essential workers like bakers, or doctors. The rest were kept imprisoned except for those unfortunates – usually the wealthier ones who the SS and the Hungarian gendarmes would pull out for interrogation and torture as they sought the whereabouts of their hidden valuables. So-called 'midwives' searched the body cavities of the interned women looking for gold and jewellery.

During that time, rumours began to circulate that the Germans intended sending them to the death camps, further fuelling the terror and sense of hopelessness. And, sure enough, at the beginning of July 1944, those fears were finally confirmed when the entire population of the ghetto was transferred to a large artificial fertiliser factory near the railroad tracks as part of the Reich plan for 'Deportation Zone V' (which included Papa). The man in charge of this operation was police captain Zoltan Papa. Later he would be sentenced to twelve years in prison by a military tribunal for his harsh treatment of the Jewish prisoners.

Escorted by gendarmes, they were forced to trudge the few hundred metres to the factory, bemused and bedraggled in our dirty. crumpled clothes that displayed the poignant yellow stars like a badge of honour. According to one eyewitness, '... they formed a long procession of people of all ages, carrying their belongings, most wearing several layers of clothing, including heavy winter wear despite the heat of summer.' All of Papa's Jews plus an additional three hundred from surrounding villages were placed in a huge shed to await their fate.

A few days later, on 4 and 5 July, the persecuted Jewish interns were herded on to two trains and deported to Auschwitz-Birkenau via the Budapest–Hatvan–Kassa route. The typically detailed German records show that a total of 2793 men, women and children were crammed on board on the cattle trucks, including a few hundred from the area surrounding Papa. Another witness said: "Only the sound of revels with gypsy music came from the railway station restaurant ... and the sobbing of victims."

A few days later, they would have arrived at the death camps. Miraculously, my mother and I were not among them. We had already escaped from the ghetto.

CHAPTER 9

Staring death in the face

HERE IS how it happened ...

Mum had a childhood friend called Janos Okolichny. He was a Christian, a lay priest in Papa who also managed the local hospital alongside my grandfather. Using funds supplied by Samu Stern, Janos had bribed the Hungarian guards to allow him into the ghetto. The intention was that all four of us – mum and I, plus Jeno and Irma – would flee in the night.

Janos led us to the southwest corner of the ghetto where Papa's main fire station stood at the corner of Bastya and Major streets. It had a front and a back entrance where we could slip through with the connivance of a fireman who Janos knew and had also bribed. Tragically, the guards got cold feet and began prevaricating; in hushed voices, Janos frantically bargained with them, and they finally agreed that mum and I could go ... but not my grandparents.

Years later, my mother was still heartbroken when she told me that the last time she saw them, they'd had a row in the shadows of the firehouse. Holding me in her arms and speaking in harsh whispers, she was adamant that she did not want to leave them behind, but they were equally adamant that she should save herself and their precious granddaughter. 'We're old, they told her. 'We've lived our lives. Now go!' And, reluctantly, tearfully, mum did – otherwise, I would not be telling this story.

I do not think my mother ever got over that traumatic moment. She loved her parents with all her heart, and it ripped her apart to abandon them. If she did not have me to protect, I truly believe she would have stayed ... and died. But that episode, in the darkness of the fire station, would haunt her for the rest of her life. I am sure it also contributed to the stroke that led to her eventual death.

It is surely not too fanciful to imagine that Jeno and Irma gave me one last, loving kiss before sadly returning to the squalor of the ghetto. They probably guessed that they would never see me, or my mother, again. Meanwhile, Janos Okolichny anxiously shepherded us to his car and drove us back to Budapest. I sometimes think about that courageous, compassionate man.

My father always maintained that Janos had had a crush on my mother since their schooldays and this had led him to risk his life for her. I do not know what happened to this heroic figure after that night, but I hope he went on to have a rich, fulfilling life. God knows he deserved it.

Earlier I mentioned the photo of me with my grandparents in Papa in 1943 when I was just a year old; it was taken on a bright, sunny day and one of the tall steeples of Saint Stephen's Catholic Church is rising up behind us. When I returned there in 2002, my husband John took another photograph of me in the same spot; the Catholic church was still fully intact behind me while the synagogue of Papa, a stone's throw away, was in ruins. That seems to me to be a sad but apt metaphor for what happened there nearly eighty years ago.

Of the 2793 innocent souls from that small, picturesque town who were put on those cattle trucks, only three hundred returned after the camps were liberated. The rest, including my grandpa and grandma, and 671 children, were butchered at Auschwitz. As I write this, I understand that there are no Jews left in Papa.

And thus, the Nazis' original, obscene objective – to make Papa 'Judenfrei' – was finally, horribly, achieved.

Believe me, it is terrifying to look at a death warrant and see your name typed on it. To know that people wanted you – an eighteen-month-old infant – to die. Yet it happened to me. It was during that return visit to Hungary in 2002 that I saw the document, picked it up in my shaking hands, goosepimples sprouting on my neck; I had not even known it existed.

It was a copy of the official Reich register that listed my grandparents, my mother and myself as among those to be deported from the Papa ghetto to Auschwitz. The original document is archived at Yad Vashem, the World Holocaust Museum in Jerusalem; the curators kindly showed it to me when I visited a few years ago.

The docket has four columns with headings in Hungarian that, from left to right, say: 'Name', 'Mother's name', 'Address' and 'Comments'. On the left-hand column, there are thirty names in alphabetical order, grouped in families, all but one name typewritten. Horizontal dotted lines separate the family groupings.

Halfway down the page, there are four entries: the first three are listed as Jeno Halasz, Irma Halasz and Erzsebet Kalmar (nee Halasz), all living at 9 Kozep Street, Papa. Below them is the fourth name: Zsuzsi Kalmar. Me. A big hand-drawn tick is entered in the fourth 'Comments' column indicating that we had been accounted for.

Interestingly, the sole hand-written entry is my mother's name. I can only deduce that she had been entered under 'K' for her married name before some eagle-eyed clerk spotted the error at the last moment and wrote in her name in ink alongside those of my grandparents and me.

When I read the copy of the deportation docket, I was sitting in the home of an elderly Jewish man with white, wispy hair called Laszlo Kiss, who lived in Papa. He was an amateur historian who had made it his life's work to scrutinise Nazi records of the Holocaust and help people like me discover the truth about their past. There is a photograph of me, straight-backed and grim-faced, watching as he pores over the Papa register before coming to the page with our names on it; Mr Kiss is colourfully dressed in a short-sleeved chequered shirt with blue and white striped braces.

We had been lucky to find Mr Kiss after visiting the Papa synagogue and finding it derelict. We knocked on the door of the nearest building and asked the woman who answered if she knew of anyone who had records of Jews from the World War Two era. She directed us to Laszlo Kiss in Vasar Street which, as it turned out, was very close to both where my grandparents had lived and the site of the 1944 ghetto.

The house was invisible from the street: it had a high fence, a lovely garden and a big wooden door. Mr Kiss and his wife had been about to go out when we arrived, but when our driver explained who we were and what we wanted, he dropped his bag and ushered us into his house. He took us into a back room which had piles of documents stacked on every surface.

Mr Kiss, who was in his nineties, told us that he had been sent to the Russian front as a 'munkaszolgat', in a slave labour battalion but had luckily survived before returning to Papa at the end of the war. From that time on, he was determined to track down and keep records of what had happened in his hometown. In his small front room, he brought out the original deportation order registry compiled by the Nazis and their Hungarian collaborators.

We spent some time poring over the thousands of names and then came the shocking moment when the old man turned to me and said, 'Here it is'. My heart turned over as I leant forward to look at the chilling historical document which essentially guaranteed the murder of my grandparents but, thankfully, as it turned out, not my mother or me. I remember going completely cold; I started to cry. Gallant Mr Kiss then stood up and hugged me.

When I looked at that document a second time, I shook my head and thought: how could these anonymous clerks have been so cold-blooded to meticulously type out the death warrants of thousands of innocent people? How did they sleep at night?

Later, I suggested to Mr Kiss that these were important documents and perhaps they should be stored somewhere safer. He said: "When I die, my son will look after them." But, a few years later, when I visited Yad Veshem, I discovered that he had sent all of them there which pleased me greatly.

All this was twenty years ago, and Mr Kiss must be dead by now, but I left a memento behind that I hope still lives to this day – I'd taken some leaves from a succulent plant from a large pot at home in Sydney with the intention of planting them somewhere in Papa. Why? Because the pot also contained the ashes of both my parents, and it just seemed to me to be a fitting tribute. Mrs Kiss kindly agreed to plant the leaves in her garden and, together, we put them in a lovely pot covered in Hungarian motifs. I still feel to this day that I had brought my mum back home.

Nowadays, I still shiver when I think back to that moment in Mr Kiss's room – seeing how close we had been to being exterminated like the great majority of Papa's Jewish community. That my mother and I were able to escape deportation and probable death was a miracle – the very stuff of a movie plot.

CHAPTER 10

The safe house on Saletrom Street

THE TIMING is exquisitely painful for me to contemplate: on 6 July 1944, just *one day* after my grandparents were taken from the Papa ghetto and loaded on to a cattle truck bound for Auschwitz, Regent Miklos Horthy suspended the round-ups and deportation of Jews following massive pressure from Western leaders including President Roosevelt and the King of Sweden.

To spell it out: their lives would have been saved if Horthy had made the decision twenty-four hours day earlier.

When our saviour Janos Okolichny had dropped Mum and I safely back in Budapest after our near-death experience in Papa, we had settled back into the downtown apartment at 19 Deak Ferenc Street with the help of our two Christian maids Borbola and her daughter Zsofia. They were Seventh Day Adventists and sympathetic to our plight; they would go on to play a major part in my personal drama a few months later.

Things had moved on from the time that we had left the city for Papa – and not for the better. Budapest had become even more a highly toxic for Jews. Their shops and businesses had been closed or transferred to new non-Jewish ownership. Times allotted for when they could shop for rationed groceries. No cars or bicycles. The hated yellow star badge, of course. On the street, Jews were harassed, asked for ID papers, and routinely arrested. Shops displayed notices in their windows that said: 'No one wearing a yellow star will be served.'

While mum and I had been in the Papa ghetto, the Mayor of Budapest, Akos Farkas, had issued a decree ordering all Jews to move to so-called 'yellow star' houses – buildings designated specifically as Jewish places of residence. The authorities demanded that the Central Jewish Council help draw up a detailed list of such places – 2,639 in total – by district, street and house number. This was published on June 16. The list included several buildings in Deak Ferenc Street, including ours. It also included Samu Stern's building at 3 Esku Street.

The city's 220,000 Jews had then been forced to leave their homes and transfer to these buildings (apart from many people like my father who were in hiding), scattered around the city and marked by a large yellow star on the front entrance. The mayoral decree had been very precise; it demanded that '... the sign shall be a six-pointed canary yellow star measuring 30 centimetres in diameter, on a 51cm x 36cm black background. This notice will be displayed at all street entrances to every house on the list. If the yellow-star sign on the house is damaged, a yellow star of the same size and colour must be painted on and maintained intact and clean at all times.'

The deadline for moving into the new abodes had been midnight on June 21, 1944; each family was allocated just one room. The mass relocation was overseen by the city police and German troops. This was a new dimension to the Endlosung programme: nothing of this sort had previously happened anywhere else in Nazi-occupied Europe. But, of course, it was designed as a temporary measure – the Jews would be moved again in November, this time into two city ghettoes – or collection centres – with the intention of deporting them to death camps, just like their country cousins before them.

All this meant that we had to share our apartment with other Jewish families who had been forced to leave their own homes.

But, given the horrors that were beginning to unfold in Budapest, this was the least of my mother's worries.

It would be three more months after we returned to Budapest before we were reunited with my father. In the meantime, I had celebrated my second birthday; there might have been candles, but I doubt there were ingredients for a cake but perhaps Zsofia had managed to scrounge a piece of chocolate for me.

Records show that, on 19 October, dad escaped from the labour camp he had been reassigned to after his stint in hospital. I don't know how he made it back to the capital but, of course, when he did arrive, he was a marked man and could not go back to our apartment. He contacted an old friend, George Olah who agreed to help him despite the danger to himself, taking him to his mother's apartment at 6 Saletrom Street, near Kozel-Rakczy Square.

George, who used to row on the Danube with my dad, had his own place a floor below in the same building, and his mother moved in with him. My mum and I then joined dad in this 'safe house', along with his brother Ferenc and his wife Gyorgi. I can picture the tears of joy and relief when he and my mother fell into each other's arms for the first time after the dramas they'd both been through in the months they'd been apart.

While researching this memoir, I checked out the apartment address on the stunning Google Street View app: the four-storey building looked derelict and in need of serious renovation; the brown stone façade was crumbling and covered in graffiti, and the front entrance to the apartments was boarded up. It probably was a fine building once, perhaps before the war, with engaged columns topped by grimacing gargoyles and ornamental wall relief sculptures, fluted stonework and ornate windows.

The street itself looked dour and narrow and, as I zoomed in to the top apartment on the fourth floor, I pictured us all hiding there seventy-five years before, with the four adults tiptoeing around, and my mother doing her best to prevent me from crying in distress or shrieking in delight and alerting neighbours to our presence.

George made sure we had enough food. Dad could not afford to be picked up in the street by the Nazis or members of the Arrow Cross, the self-proclaimed national socialist party, because, as an escaped slave labourer, he would have been summarily shot, or perhaps worse, taken to the nearby Gestapo headquarters at the Astoria Hotel, tortured and never seen again. As one witness said of the time: "Everything was breaking down. You could go outside to buy bread and be shot to death."

Then there was the added danger of bombs dropping on the city; these came from American planes from Italian bases which had started hitting targets in Budapest in April that same year. On 2 July, more than five hundred Allied bombers had hit two train stations, followed by further attacks on 14 July, 27 July and 30 July on industrial sites and oil refineries. The aerial onslaught killed thousands of civilians and added to the general climate of fear in the city, as residents – Jews and Gentiles alike, huddled in dark, dank basement shelters. We couldn't do that, of course.

But then, disaster struck. My mother later told me that, after six weeks in hiding, a neighbour in the building heard a toilet flush and warned George Olah that intruders might have gained entry to the supposedly empty apartment. In case, the neighbour informed blabbed to the Gestapo, my father decided that it would be safer for everyone, including his friend George, if we moved out. The latter had already done more than most: in Budapest during those days, most Christians had already pushed their former Jewish friends into what could be described as a 'social ghetto' – at best pretending they did not exist, at worst betraying them to their persecutors.

Almost immediately, saddened and scared, we headed back to

Deak Ferenc Street in the dead of night despite the curfew. I'm guessing my mother would have been holding one hand over my mouth to hush me; if the soldiers patrolling the streets had seen or heard us, we could have been shot on the spot.

CHAPTER 11

Heroes and villains

WHEN MUM and I arrived back in Budapest, two very different men, for quite different reasons, were proving to be beacons of hope to the city's Jewish community. And both had strong connections to my mother's 'bacsi', Samu Stern, who would have been relieved that his part in the plot to have us freed from the Papa ghetto had paid off. I have no doubt that mum would have found some way to thank him personally for saving our lives.

The first was Raoul Wallenberg. A former businessman, he was working with the US War Refugee Board when he was sent to Budapest in July 1944 as a special envoy, attached to the Swedish Legation. On arrival, he visited the Jewish Council's offices in Sip Street to present a letter of introduction from Sweden's Chief Rabbi, Dr Marcus Ehrenpreis to Samu Stern. Wallenberg was briefed on the increasingly dire situation facing Hungary's Jewry. The Germans had, by then, already sent more than 400,000 from the provinces to their deaths. Budapest's Jews now faced a similar threat.

Wallenberg immediately went to work. With the help of other foreign diplomats like Carl Lutz, the Swiss consul general, he began distributing 'protective passports' which meant that hard-pressed Jews facing arrest or deportation could claim Swedish citizenship. Others were placed in buildings designated as Swedish territory. Every day, the Swedish envoy himself faced arrest or assassination as he dealt with those on both sides of the Jewish issue, including Adolf Eichmann and Samu Stern, and later the Arrow Cross.

Wallenberg once explained his selfless actions thus: "To me there's no other choice. I've accepted the assignment and I could never return to Stockholm without the knowledge that I'd done everything in human power to save as many Jews as possible."

It is estimated that the Swedish hero indeed saved many thousands of Jewish men, women and children from 'vernichtungslager' (extermination), in the months before the Red Army laid siege to Budapest later that same year. But, shortly after the city was liberated in January 1945, Wallenberg was summoned to a meeting by the commander of the Soviet forces. He was never seen again. It is widely believed that he was accused of espionage, transported to Moscow and later executed in the Lubyanka, although some reports dispute that.

Monuments to this inspirational character still proliferate around the world; hundreds, if not thousands of schools, streets and institutions bear his name. In 2013, for example, the then Governor-General, Quentin Bryce bestowed Australia's first posthumous Honorary Citizenship Award to the Swedish humanitarian.

The second man to offer some hope to the beleaguered Jewry of Budapest (or, more accurately, a select number of them) was Rudolf Kasztner, a Jewish journalist and lawyer who also had links to the Stern family. Kasztner was a forceful Zionist activist who dreamt of creating a Jewish homeland in Palestine. Unlike the more modest, self-effacing Wallenberg, he was a polarising figure both during, and after, the war; some regarded him as a 'snobbish intellectual' while others saw him as 'selfless and willing to take risks for his beliefs'.

All agreed, however, that he was a powerful advocate for Jews and a consummate political fixer; there's little doubt he brought those skills when he moved to Budapest in 1941 from his home city Kolozsvar (now Cluj) in Transylvania. There, in 1943, Kasztner helped set up the Relief and Rescue Committee, also known as 'Va'ada', along with other Zionists, to help Jewish refugees fleeing to Hungary from neighbouring occupied countries to escape the Nazi oppression.

The following year, in April 1944, against the backdrop of the Nazi's brutal oppression of Hungary's Jewry, he began negotiating with Adolf Eichmann and his cohorts on a controversial so-called 'blood for goods' plan that would see doomed Jews exchanged for military hardware and trucks. It sounds stranger than fiction, but, in June, Kasztner managed to persuade Eichmann to allow almost seventeen hundred Hungarian Jews to escape deportation to Auschwitz in return for an agreed ransom. Instead, they would be sent on a special train to freedom in Switzerland.

A committee was set up to select the lucky passengers; it included Kasztner himself, as well as Samu Stern and other Jewish leaders; they also collected the ransom and reports suggest that this was paid in gold, diamonds and currency as well as stocks and shares to the tune of around US$1000 per person. Among those selected to board the train were senior rabbis, Zionist leaders, members of the Jewish intelligentsia, and Kasztner's friends and family – a total of 1,684 passengers. Included on the list was the Bamberger family – parents Rozsi and Gyuri and their nineteen-year-old daughter Lidia.

Rozsi was the daughter of Samu Stern, and my mother knew her well. At that time, Rozsi was forty-four, her daughter Lidia just nineteen and my mother thirty, so it's unlikely that they were close given the age differences. But the two families mixed at social events and visited each other's homes. It's even possible that my mother, given Samu Stern's affection for her, might have been offered the opportunity to leave on the train with the Bambergers, but of course, my father was stuck in the labour camp and my mother would not have left without him.

The 'Kasztner Train', as it became known, consisting of thirty-five cattle cars, left Budapest on 30 June 1944. According to reports, the passengers were allowed to bring with them two changes of clothing, six sets of underwear, and food for ten days.

After the war, when he had emigrated to Israel, Kasztner would be accused of 'selling his soul to the devil' and personally profiting from his deal with Eichmann. In 1954, a high-profile libel trial in Israel saw him accused of collaborating with the Nazis, favouring friends and family (including his mother and brother) with regards to passage on the train, and of not doing enough to warn Hungarian Jews about their fate.

Kasztner sensationally lost the case – the Israeli Supreme Court would exonerate him a few years later – but not before Hungary's 'Oskar Schindler' had met with a sticky end, just like his Swedish counterpart Raoul Wallenberg. He was assassinated in Tel Aviv on March 3, 1957, by right-wing Israeli nationalists. Since then, the Kasztner controversy has been the subject of several books and a documentary film.

These were two men from vastly different backgrounds and with different strategies, but united in their aims to save human beings. But, while Wallenberg is universally lauded as a humanitarian and hero, the more colourful Kasztner polarises opinion as to whether he was a hero or villain.

But for all his undoubted flaws, no one can dispute that the man displayed incredible ingenuity and courage – imagine him sitting across the table from a psychopath like Adolf Eichmann, playing a life-or-death game of poker. Remember, he would have been eyeballing the monster who was already responsible for the extermination of millions of Jews. As he once said, while being verbally abused at a meeting of the Jewish Council: "Do you really think we could just stand up and leave the Gestapo's table anytime we wanted to? So why don't you put your head into the lion's mouth instead?"

The surviving Jews on the Kasztner Train like Rozsi Bamberger, and their descendants, were unequivocal: to them, he was most definitely a hero, albeit a tragic one. As *Yad Vashem* chairman Joseph Lapid, himself a Hungarian holocaust survivor, said in 2007: 'There was no man in the history of the Holocaust who saved more Jews and was subjected to more injustice than Kasztner.'

While on the subject of heroes, I feel it would be remiss of me if I did not mention two women whose bravery during that traumatic time was truly breathtaking.

First, Marta Haas who had lived near us in Deak Ferenc Street in Budapest during the war. I was shocked to learn decades later that she had worked for the Hungarian Resistance. At the time, she was a very attractive girl in her late teens; she would hang out in the city's bars and chat up Gestapo officers before taking them to a dark alley with the promise of sex – there members of the resistance would kill the Germans.

This incredible woman later received a medal for her bravery from the Hungarian government, before emigrating to Melbourne. Dad and I stayed at her house when we visited for the 1956 Olympics; I thought she was the most stunning and stylish woman with the most amazing wardrobe. By then I was roughly the same age as she had been when she acted as a 'honeytrap' for the resistance, and I could see how she would have made the perfect femme fatale. But it was hard to imagine how she had found the inner strength to do what she did. Even all these years later I am still in awe of her heroism.

Then there was Hannah Szenes, born in Budapest in 1921, who emigrated to Israel when she was 18. Concerned with the plight of Europe's Jewry, the young poet decided to join the British army in 1942. She and four Jewish men in her special commando unit then parachuted into Yugoslavia in March 1944 to fight alongside Tito's partisans. She then crossed alone into Hungary on June 9, three months after the German occupation to do what she could to help the country's Jews.

Hannah was captured at the border with a radio transmitter on her way to Budapest where her mother was still living. She was held for five months and brutally tortured but refused to give up the radio codes used to communicate with the resistance and the British. In October, she was convicted of treason by a secret Arrow Cross court and executed by a firing squad soon after. The young heroine who was just 23 years old when she was martyred once famously said: "Even if they catch me, the Jews will be notified. They will know that at least one person tried to reach them."

In Israel, Hannah Szenes has long been regarded as a national hero; her body was exhumed in Budapest in 1950 and reburied in the military cemetery at Mount Herzl in Jerusalem. But it took many more than fifty years before Hungarian authorities finally named a tiny park after her a few blocks away from Andrassy Street.

It was the very least they could do.

CHAPTER 12

Ticket to freedom

ROZSI BAMBERGER was the younger of Samu Stern's two daughters. The other girl, Irma, who was forty-eight at the time, was married to a doctor, Endre Elek; they had decided to remain in Budapest with their children, Maria and Andras, and her father, when the 'tickets' for the Kasztner Train journey were offered to all the Stern family.

Despite extensive efforts, I've not been able to find out much more about Irma, other than that her son Andras went to Canada after the 1956 revolution, while Maria came to Australia about the same time.

But I struck lucky when I found that Rozsi, who was forty-four when she boarded the train on 30 June 1944, with her husband Gyuri Bamberger, a civil servant, and their daughter Lidia, had written a detailed diary about the whole experience and this provided me with some filtered insights into her life and her character. "We were the among the privileged ones," she wrote, "who had a little hope to survive."

In her diary, which was later published* in 2012 with the title – *From Budapest to Bergen-Belsen: A notebook from 1944* – she describes the lead-up to the decision to go:

> "One day my father told us that if we wanted to leave Budapest, there would be one more opportunity to make Aliyah (immigrate to Palestine) with the Zionists. Gyuri, without any hesitation, decided to take the trip, even though this was also very dangerous."

The remarkable diary consists of just forty-four neatly handwritten pages in a blue-covered, lined notebook that detail the events beginning with the German occupation on 19 March 1944 up to the family's arrival in Switzerland six months later. The man who published it, Zsolt Zagoni, a lovely man who proved very helpful to me when we were researching the Stern family, described it thus: "The importance of the notebook is that an everyday person, realising the extraordinariness of the events, decides to tell her story, her fate, and the drama of her family's life during the black weeks and months in Hungary while she tries to understand the incomprehensible."

This is how Rozsi describes the day of the Nazi invasion:

> "On this Sunday, news that the Germans have occupied Budapest has spread like wildfire. People, especially Jews, are in unimaginable fear and shock. We have so far only heard from the radio and from stories of survivors about the brutalities of German terror and now we feel that the Jewish community in Hungary is facing the same fate. Already on the first day, some of the Jewish gentlemen holding the most prestigious positions were interned. They came twice to our house, and to the Community on Sip Street, looking for my father.
>
> "My father wanted to buy time, so our whole family spent the entire day and night with one of our doctor relatives. This is where we were notified that Obersturmbannfuhrer Krumey had ordered all the community leaders, including priests, principals, and the president, to be present in the Sip Street office at 10 o' clock on Monday. We begged my father not to go, as we were afraid he would be interned too. He said he would not hide and no matter what happens he would go to the indicated place. I cannot describe how nervous we were. Irma spent all morning walking up

and down Sip Street, so at least she would see if my dad was taken by the Germans."

Rozsi, who was born Rozalia Stern in 1901, in Janoshaza – the small town where her father had attended a yeshiva in his youth, describes how the Germans formed the eight-man Jewish Council with her dad as president and how they were made responsible for ensuring the new anti-Jewish regulations would be carried out properly, thus saving the Israelite community from atrocities.

Her notes from that day are eerily prescient as she discerns "cruelty and lies behind the smooth manners." Nevertheless, I find it hard to grasp how shocked she and her family must have been at the speed and ferocity of the tsunami of terror that hit the city almost overnight ...

> "One of their first moves was to have all Jewish phones cut off. Then radios had to be turned in. Whole warehouses and private properties had to be placed at their disposal within 24 hours. Jewish stores were closed and their goods confiscated. All business transactions were paralysed and all you could see were worried, terrified people. Relatives, friends and acquaintances all turned to the president [Samu Stern]. What would happen now? What fate is waiting for us? We always looked at my dad as a superior creature for his intelligence and kindness. Now I remember, with tears of emotion, how heroically he comforted and encouraged everybody and suppressed his anxiety and worries for his own children and grandchildren ... even the Germans were impressed by his brave and calm behaviour ..."

Remember, this was just the first few days of the occupation. But Eichmann and his henchmen had arrived with a detailed plan, and they wasted no time in executing it. As a result, things were soon going to get a good deal worse for the Jews of Budapest ...

"People began to be collected from the streets. For example, if a married woman or a young woman went to the store or men left for work, you never knew if they would see their families again. Or would be captured on the street. At night, men and women were taken from their homes. The yellow star had to be worn ... a lot of people were afraid to go out like this, branded. Many chose to commit suicide."

These horrible events contributed to the Bambergers' difficult decision to accept the offer of seats on the Kasztner Train despite the consequence of leaving both her father and her husband's eighty-year-old mother behind.

At the time, the Bambergers were living in Samu Stern's apartment in Esku Street along with Rozsi's father and five others – probably Irma, her husband and children. Samu's wife Poldina had died previously in 1937 from coronary disease and diabetes; her death certificate said she was sixty-one, yet the gravestone she shares with her husband and her daughter Rozsi has her birth in 1870, making her sixty-six when she died. I cannot explain the discrepancy.

The Stern home was often used for meetings with Jewish leaders and city businessmen. Rozsi said that Rudolph Kasztner visited there on 29 June and tried to persuade her father, who was then aged seventy, to leave because, he said, "If there are no mice, there is no need for a cat either."

Kasztner told them all that he had a firm promise that they would reach their destination and the best proof of this was that his own family would be on the train. Stern, however, refused to leave. He is reported to have said around that time that he the idea of abandoning the sinking ship was "unimaginable".

On 30 June, Stern, accompanied by the German soldier billeted in his apartment, took his daughter's family and their luggage by taxi to the Arena Street synagogue where the Kasztner passengers were assembling. There they waited anxiously for hours in pouring rain with hundreds of others before the train arrived. Here is how Rozsi describes the scene:

> "We sat (in the open carriages) lined around the sides, squeezed against each other, our legs hanging down. On both sides there were German soldiers ... people on the street gathered in groups wondering where all these yellow-starred Jews were being taken."

The train then departed for what they believed would be Switzerland at 10am on Saturday, 1 July 1944.

> "There were seventy-two of us in our wagon ... it was only supposed to hold six horses or forty people. We were sitting on our blankets, as tightly packed as we could be. There were twenty-six children in our wagon including sixteen orphans. It was a miserable scene ... it had no toilet, of course so our human needs could only be taken care of when the train stopped for a while, and we got permission to get off. People jumped off the train like animals and shamelessly took care of their needs."

The train passed through the Austrian border, skirting the suburbs of Vienna and then on to the town of Linz, where the exhausted passengers were ordered to disembark. According to the lists, there were 972 women and 712 men.

Rozsi writes of the humiliation and terror inflicted on them by the guards, of how they were taken to a military delousing station for medical inspections and showers; there they were forced to strip and stand naked for hours waiting to see medical personnel or go into the showers. The terrified women were subjected to intimate examinations by the doctors, supposedly in a search for lice; they also had their heads and pubic areas shaved.

On 9 July, a Sunday and more than a week after they'd left Budapest, the train arrived at a place called Bergen-Belsen, infamous as the place where Anne Frank died. None of the passengers had heard of it and were soon shocked to find out that it was another death camp. The Magyar passengers were taken to a special section of the Bergen-Belsen camp which would become known as the 'Ungarnlager' (Hungarian camp) with its own barracks.

A couple of weeks later, the first batch of 318 Kasztner passengers were sent to neutral Switzerland, arriving on 18 August 1944. A second, larger group of approximately 1350 passengers had to wait until December until they could follow. Incredibly, Krasztner's proud boast to Samu Stern that the great train escape would be successful turned out to be true.

Rozsi, Gyuri and Lidia all returned to Budapest at war's end. Rozsi died in 1953, aged just fifty-two, a year after her husband. Despite being ill for some time (which her mother blamed on the long, agonising ordeal they'd endured) Lidia married her fiancé Pal Sas in October 1945, and they had two sons, Istvan and Peter.

I very much regret that I never met Lidia or her family, but I was able to correspond with her granddaughter Anna Sas who kindly helped with some research. I've seen just three photographs of Lidia, one taken in 1961 when she would have been thirty-four, and the others taken when she was much older. They show a handsome woman with a high forehead, a warm smile and a look of intelligence. I bet she had some stories to tell! Not only did she survive the perilous train journey but then, just when she thought it was safe, she would then have had to endure the stifling suppression of the Soviet era.

* Edited and published by Zsolt Zagoni and translated (from Hungarian) into English by Gabor and Carolyn Banfalvi.

CHAPTER 13

A desperate family under siege

AS ROZSI and her family were eking out a miserable existence in the Bergen-Belsen death camp, things were only slightly better in Budapest. After the scare at the safe house, we were now holed up in our apartment in Deak Ferenc Street – not in its comfortable living rooms and bedrooms, but in the small, cold and dark crawl space above the bathroom where the luggage was kept. We remained there during daylight hours, only venturing down below after dusk.

It was now early November 1944. The situation outside was becoming increasingly desperate. The Red Army had entered Hungary weeks before and was pressing towards the capital city. Adolf Eichmann had already fled, but Arrow Cross thugs were running rampant in the street, murdering and robbing Jews. I still have a rugged stainless-steel army knife that my father kept with him at all times in the luggage space as a weapon. He once said: 'If they'd found us, I'd planned to take at least one of them out.' Typical of dad.

The two maids, Borbala and her daughter Zsofia, continued to show remarkable loyalty and empathy, smuggling in a meagre supply of food for us, including a case of apples. "They were saints," my mother told me. "If not for them, we would not have survived." A decade later, when we were adjusting to life in Australia, she used to send them clothes and other gifts. As I write this, I think of those two women with immense gratitude for their kindness, and with awe at their bravery. If the Nazis or the Arrow Cross fascists had become aware that they were aiding Jewish fugitives, the mother and daughter would have been arrested and probably killed.

As you can imagine, life in a small, cramped space amongst the suitcases and the collection of bric-a-brac that all families hoard was no picnic but, compared to the hell our fellow Jews were enduring in the increasingly scary streets of the city, it was heaven. As both the Allies and the Red Army were making headway against the Axis powers, the German grip on Budapest began to weaken. A month before, Regent Micklos Horthy had negotiated a ceasefire with the Russians and ordered Hungarian troops to lay down their arms.

The Reich responded in typically brutal fashion on October 16 by orchestrating a coup: the Nazis forced Horthy to abdicate while taking him and his family into 'protective custody' in Germany. It was then that they did something so callous and cruel that it would destroy any remaining shred of hope that Budapest's Jews might have had that they would survive – Hitler appointed Ferenc Szalasi, the leader of the fascist, ultranationalist Arrow Cross party, as Prime Minister of Hungary. The party's name came from its logo – a white circle containing a green square cross ending in arrows on all sides.

It is hard to overstate the hammer blow that this was to the remaining Jewish community, already hanging on to survival and sanity by its fingernails. After all they had endured in the six months since the German occupation began, this was a crushing, catastrophic turn of events.

Immediately, Szalasi's thugs – many of them recruited from the ranks of convicted criminals – acted like a pack of devil dogs taken off the leash, snarling and salivating as they launched a reign of unspeakable terror in Budapest against the already hard-pressed Jewry. In just a few short months, they drafted thousands into forced labour gangs; then, in early November, they concentrated more than seventy-thousand men, women and children in the Ujlaki brickyards in Obuda (not far from the Aquincum Hotel where I stayed decades later) before forcing them to march on foot to camps in Austria. Thousands died along the way, either shot by their captors or succumbing to the winter conditions and starvation.

A Red Cross official who had visited the brickworks was staggered by what he saw: '... five or six thousand starving Jewish prisoners in the open yard, soaked to the skin and frozen to the marrow. Some who had committed suicide lay on the ground.'

On 29 November a decree proclaimed that the remaining Budapest Jews must enter the newly created ghetto near the Dohany Street synagogue. More of this later. It was also at this time that the Arrow Cross also started grabbing Jews off the streets and taking them to the banks of the Danube before shooting them and dumping their bodies in the icy river. These same brutes raided the 'csillagos hazak', or yellow-star houses, stealing valuables, shooting men in the courtyards and assaulting women and girls. It was not safe for any Jew to be outside in the streets.

Meanwhile, as if all this terror was not enough, Budapest was also suffering widespread bombing as the Russians began to lay siege to the city.

As I said earlier, we were comparatively lucky: we had shelter, just enough to eat and, despite the constant fear of an Arrow Cross raid, we were safe. Outside, it was a different story: the shattering sounds of heavy Soviet ordinance smashing buildings to bits and the seemingly endless cacophony of police and ambulance sirens, was a constant backdrop, and the small window high on the sloping eave wall showed an angry red and orange glow and rising plumes of dust and smoke every night. My mother once told me that two things kept her awake: the appalling noise of war and a constant, all-consuming terror that I would be killed by shells hitting our apartment block.

Obviously, we could not simply go down to one of the bomb shelters for safety. I sometimes imagine my mum and dad, huddled together for warmth in the gloomy crawl space, whispering so as not to give our presence away to anyone else in the building, as they ceaselessly discussed what they should do. In the end, given the threat of shelling, the increasing lack of food and the severe drop in temperatures as winter began, they made the gut-wrenching decision to send me away from the city.

With heavy hearts, they negotiated with our maids, asking them to take me to the safety of their relatives' house in a village near the city of Miskolc, about 150km north of Budapest. Amid the nightmarish chaos in the city streets, they knew it would have been too dangerous for them as Jews to take me – the chances of them being spotted and arrested was high, given the marauding bands of Arrow Cross – and, if they were caught, I would certainly die also. At the very least, we would be taken to the ghetto. Bottom line – they thought I'd have a much better chance of survival in the care of the maids' family. So, along with our hidden cash, jewellery and other family valuables, Borbola and Zsofia set out with me in their arms to the railway station. It was mid-November 1944.

Can you imagine my parents' anguish as they kissed their precious baby for the last time, not knowing if they would survive to see me again? For mum it was particularly poignant as it reprised the moment in the Papa ghetto, five months before, when she had said goodbye to her own parents, Irma and Jeno.

Postscript: After the war, many Arrow Cross leaders were captured and tried for war crimes and more than six thousand indictments for murder were served against Arrow Cross men in just a few months. Some Arrow Cross officials were executed, including Ferenc Szalasi.

Interestingly, I discovered that, decades later, a senior AC man was tracked down to Melbourne in Australia. He had long been on a wanted list by the Magyar authorities for 'suspected genocide', and the famous Nazi hunters, the Simon Wiesenthal Centre, was also hot on his heels. In 2006, Lajos Polgar, formerly Jozsef Kardos, was indicted by the Australian Government for war crimes. Unfortunately, he died before he could be put on trial.

And another alleged Nazi war criminal, Karoly Steiner, accused of killing a young Jewish man in Budapest in November 1944, was discovered living in Western Australia and arrested on 8 July 2005 by Federal Police. He was living under the assumed name Charles Zentai. He had been listed on the Simon Wiesenthal Centre's list of most wanted Nazi war criminals.

Efforts to extradite Steiner dragged on for years until he died, aged 96, in 2017. What chilled me when reading about him was the fact that he had arrived in Australia by sea around the same time as I did. It is even possible we were on the same ship.

CHAPTER 14

The Hungarian Hamlet

EVEN IN the age of the internet, our family friend Samu Stern remains a surprisingly enigmatic figure. There are surprisingly few personal details to be found about the man who, during that terrible year of 1944, walked a tense, tortuous tightrope between the obscene demands of the occupying Nazi leaders and the desperate fears of the Jewish population.

But, while there are reams of dusty material about his activities with the Central Jewish Council and his dealings with Eichmann and his cronies, including detailed minutes of the meetings they had in their Budapest offices at 12 Sip Street, remarkably little info exists about the man himself.

The many excellent books about the Hungarian Holocaust invariably mention the president of the Judenrat, but the only book devoted specifically to Stern is the one he wrote himself: *Emlekirataim – Versenyfutas az idovel!* (My memoir – Race Against Time!), dictated to his secretary in 1946 but not published until 2004; and that largely confines itself to a defensive self-justification of his actions during that unprecedented moment in history. He dedicated the book to his grandchildren saying it could provide valuable lessons, and insights into his role and involvement in the history of the holocaust. "Take this book with love, and be wiser for it," he says.

In it, Stern also talks eloquently about his love for his wife of nearly forty-five years, Leopoldina, and her unquestioning loyalty and support. "She asked to be part of my life, and she was part of my life throughout all my left to right leanings, my good and bad times,' he says. 'She never criticised me and did not question my decisions."

Even Yad Vashem, Israel's official memorial to the victims of the Holocaust, which has an impressive historical archive (and has been extremely helpful to me), carries little about a man who suddenly and inexplicably found himself having to deal on a day-to-day basis with key figures of the Hungarian Holocaust like Regent Miklos Horthy, Raoul Wallenberg, Rudolph Kasztner and Adolf Eichmann in the middle of "… probably the greatest and most horrible crime ever committed in the whole history of the world," as Churchill put it.

So, given his connection to my family, and the generous help he gave to my parents, I will set out what little more I've been able to glean about him during my months of research for this memoir. Despite that stated connection, I will endeavour to paint an impartial picture of a man who, up until March 1944, was living comfortably and contentedly, secure in the knowledge that he had been highly successful in his career, had provided wonderfully for his family and was highly respected in the wider community. Here goes …

Stern was not an imposing figure: probably the smallest man in the room at any time, but then again, possibly the smartest. With his tiny frame, large ears, balding head fringed by white hair and soft, dark big eyes, he looks a little like a Yiddish Yoda. In the few photographs that exist in the public domain, his face invariably has a serious but benign cast, his gaze solemn and steady but conveying little about what he was thinking, like a professional poker player. It might be my imagination, but when looking at his photographs, I detect a quiet sadness about the man, perhaps due to the dark circles around his eyes and the slightly pursed mouth.

Yad Vashem gives his birthplace as Janoshaza but several other sources suggest it was actually the nearby town of Nemesszalok, and that he later went to a yeshiva, or religious school, in the former town. Both places, as I've mentioned before, are very close to Papa where my mother's family lived. And it is probable that Stern was a friend of my grandfather Jeno Halasz. At any rate, he was born on 5 January 1874, the son of peasant farmers Lipot Stern and Fani Hoffmann who also ran a small grocery store. Against his parents' wishes, he would leave the fields behind him as his brilliant career took off, first in the food/dairy industry, then in the more rarefied world of banking.

During the First World War, he ran a refrigeration company; he was also a director of the Hungarian Commercial Bank of Pest and helped control the army's food supply during the war for which he was honoured by King Franz Josef of Hungary (and Emperor of Austria) with the title of 'Hofrat', or Counselor to the Royal Court.

Around 1894, Samu married Leopoldina 'Poldina' Reisz. Photographs from the pre-war period show her to be a matronly woman with grey, wavy hair and round spectacles. Like her husband, she was active in the Jewish community and was president of the National Association of Hungarian Jewish Women's Associations (MINOSZ) in Hungary. Poldina regarded needlework as very important in the education of women and, between 1932 and her death in 1937, she crocheted a set of thirty-two decorative pieces for the Great Synagogue in Dohany Street. According to press reports at the time, these were consecrated at a ceremony witnessed by more than ten thousand people. Pieces of the collection still belong to the synagogue but are no longer in use.

As I have mentioned previously, the Sterns had two daughters Irma and Rozsi. Irma's daughter Maria was called 'Marika' by the family, and I came across a reference to her in a book which serves as a pointer to her grandfather's character. Apparently, instead of a handsome gift on her birthday in November, Samu and Poldina would, each year, pay for a party at the girls' orphanage run by the Jewish Women's Association in Budapest, attended by two hundred of its occupants. This was in the early to mid-thirties.

Before the war, the Sterns lived at 28 Nador Street in the Uj-Lipotvaros district, a leafy, tree-lined street with elegant, light coloured stone buildings close to the Parliament and the Magyar-Nemzeti Bank, and Liberty Square; only three minutes from where the 'Shoes on the Danube Bank' memorial is now located. The four-storey building, with high, double oak doors, is now home to the Fovarosi Torvenyszek Cegbirosaga Budapest – the Metropolitan Court of Registration.

Later, the family moved to the spacious apartment at 3 Esku Street in what was then Budapest's Fourth District, not far from my parents' home where Stern would host meetings of senior government ministers and prominent businessmen. The original street was the gateway to the Erzsebet Bridge which was blown up by retreating German troops in January 1945. Esku Street then disappeared when the bridge was completely rebuilt, although there is now a street on the Buda side with that name.

In the mid-thirties, Stern's attention had begun to focus on service to the Jewish community, at first in Budapest, but then the whole of Hungary, as president of the Hungarian Israelite National Office. He rubbed shoulders with the country's great and the good, including industrialists, senior politicians and power-brokers; he is reported to have been playing cards with the Regent in his official residence in Buda Castle when a call came from Adolf Hitler's HQ inviting the Regent to Schloss Klessheim to discuss, among other things, the 'Jewish question'.

It was precisely that unique position of power and influence at the centre of Hungary's elite that meant he was almost inevitably the go-to person when SS captains Hermann Krumey and Dieter Wisliceny arrived at the offices at Sip Street on 19 March 1944 and demanded the formation of a Judenrat (in Hungarian – Zsido Tanacs) to help them do their dirty work.

"I was singled out by the Germans," Stern says in his book. "I was directed." The timing was ironic – their arrival coincided with the Jewish holiday of Purim, which celebrates the defeat of an attempted genocide of the Jews of the Persian Empire in the fifth century BC. "Although the two SS officers were civil, neither I nor other leaders were fooled – we knew something of how the Germans had behaved in other parts of central Europe," he said.

But in his wildest nightmares, Samu Stern could not have envisaged what was to come, the horror that would soon unfold. The next six months would prove to the most hellish, sickening, soul-sapping period of his life, while the Jews of Hungary would suffer unimaginable and unrelenting horror.

Hermann Krumey gave a hint of what was to come when, at the first meeting, he declared: "From now on all the affairs of the Jews of Hungary are under the jurisdiction of the Sondereinsatzkommando of the SS."

Stern says that he and his new council colleagues were also told that, if they did not obey, they would be considered saboteurs and 'kivegszik' – finished off. Horrified, the Jewish leaders turned to their friends and contacts in the highest levels of the Hungarian government that same night, only to be told: "Do whatever the Germans tell you."

The seven-member Judenrat was charged with governing the Jewish population (which meant largely keeping them ignorant of the Final Solution, and soothing their fears), communicating the numerous anti-Semitic decrees issued by the Germans, and administering their demands, including closure of shops, curfews and the set-up of ghettoes. As Stern says in his book, "A kocka el volt vetr'" – "The dice was thrown."

So, why did he accept the job? It's clear from his writings that Stern felt he had no choice: if he had refused, he would find himself and his family imprisoned or murdered. What is also clear is that he also believed that he was the best person to do it, and do it in such a way that he could somehow soften the hammer blows that the Nazis would rain down on the Jews in Hungary, but also slow their impact until the war's end: "Could I abdicate responsibility for my people at this time when I had so much experience in leadership?"

He also knew that if he didn't do it, someone else would – perhaps someone who would cause more death and destruction for the Jewish people. Hubris perhaps, but it's probably the way Stern saw it. This is what he said: "A prisoner at the mercy of his jailer is not in a position to object to the cell into which he is thrown. It is not good for the flock to change an experienced shepherd for an inexperienced one who just happened to be accepted in the midst of a tempest."

He and the other council members believed both that the war would end within months and, in the meantime, that the Hungarian Government would help them. As it turned out, they were sadly mistaken in this strategy, but I sincerely believe they had the best intentions of their community at heart. Many, but not all, including Stern, could have escaped from Hungary to safety, but chose to remain and do what they could to delay deportations and keep the Israelites from panicking. So, they made their decision and accepted the task. In the end, as one historian put it, it may be that they decided badly because it was impossible to decide better. Or they that were in what some ethicists describe as a "world of competing sorrows".

Yet, while Stern may have cooperated with the Germans – he'd no doubt totally reject the word 'collaborated', he was no puppet. In the years he served the Jewish community in an official capacity, he constantly spoke out against the growing anti-Semitism in Hungary and denounced the communists' theory of an 'international Jewish conspiracy'.

And let's not forget that Stern himself was not immune from the hostile attentions of the Nazis. On 18 August 1944, he was arrested by the Gestapo, along with his family, and taken in the middle of the night to one of their interrogation centres in the Buda Hills. Then they were locked up in the Pest County jail before being released the next day after Regent Horthy had intervened.

Two main charges have been laid against Samu Stern and the other Jewish leaders about their actions during that terrible time: first that they collaborated with the Nazis, and second, that they withheld their growing knowledge of both Auschwitz and the Endlosung from their fellow Jews. Stern himself was accused of the former after the war, but he died before any prosecution ensued.

With regard to the second charge, it was certainly true that in 1944 he and the others were fully aware of what was happening at the death camps. Ample evidence proves that. Stern himself admitted as much n his memoir: "... I knew what they had done in all the occupied countries in Central Europe, and I knew their operation was a long series of murders and looting."

Stern always claimed the council members did not want to alert their fellow Jews to this appalling truth because they would panic and, in turn, this would accelerate the dire consequences. God knows how this solemn, careful man slept at night, while refusing to communicate the horrors of Auschwitz. As one historian put it: "Their goodwill was beyond doubt but eventually they became the obedient instruments of the Nazi extermination policy. This was their tragedy."

When Ferenc Szalasi and his fascist Arrow Cross party, with German backing, seized control of the government in mid-October 1944, Stern went into hiding; if the fascists found him, he would be a dead man. The stress and strain of that period – remarkably, just seven months from 19 March until 15 October – on both his health and mental state must have been immense and probably contributed to his death just a year after the war's end on June 8, 1946.

Between those times, some Jews called for his prosecution, saying Stern was a Nazi collaborator who betrayed all Hungarian Jewry in exchange for the lives of himself and his family and friends, but he was not charged after a police investigation.

So, hero or villain? In the end, while conflicted about his actions, I have come to the view that Samu Stern was akin to a Shakespearean tragic character: a Hungarian Hamlet perhaps, feted and flattered as a businessman and Jewish leader – a King's counsellor, no less – for most of his life and career, a principled man who had worked valiantly for his family and community, he was finally, horribly, forced into a desperate role not of his choosing, a dreadful dilemma that would try and test him and, ultimately, negate much of the good he had done in his life.

As the noted Holocaust historian Professor R. L. Braham wrote: "Stern still attempted everything in his power under the circumstances and given his own background, tradition and experience, to save whatever he could …" Braham also confirmed that Stern had been offered the opportunity to leave Hungary by a fellow member of the Judenrat but had refused.

From all of this I think we can deduce that Samu Stern, despite his humble beginnings, was a high achiever, an intelligent man, ambitious and proud of both his success as a businessman and his prominence in, and contribution to, the wider Jewish community. He was clearly loved by his family. But he was also flawed: his utter confidence in his own cleverness and the rigidity of his belief that he was the best man to manage what then was a uniquely perilous situation speaks to both courage and conceit.

By the time Stern began dictating his memoirs to his secretary in the later months of 1945, I fancy that he was less sure of his actions – his tone is a mix of defiance, defensiveness and denial. This is reflected in one of his assertions: "He who could have done something else, more and better in those times, in that hard position, should cast the first stone at us."

But then again, he might just have had a point. And this man helped my family in the direst of circumstances not once, not twice but three times, so I'm going to give him the benefit of the doubt.

I still try, and fail, to imagine that small, serious, solemn Jew sitting across from the tall, thin, sneering uber-Nazi Adolf Eichmann with his cruel lips, long nose and death skull uniform, knowing full well that the monster had already been responsible for millions of murders, and keenly aware also that the SS officer could click his fingers and he, Stern, would be on the next transport to Auschwitz.

How did he feel when he met with the monster at Sip Street or Eichmann's HQ in the Majestic Hotel on the Buda side of the Danube? How did he manage to compose himself? What went through his mind while sitting there? Who did he talk to about his fears and revulsion? His wife Poldina was no longer there to confide in having passed away several years before. That was probably a blessing in disguise – at least she escaped the horror and heartache of that time, and the stress of living with her husband's impossible situation.

Again, I fervently wish I had talked to my mother in more depth about her 'bacsi', and whether she or my father ever discussed these issues with him or his family. Was she sympathetic, or was she simply stunned by the consequences of his actions? I'll never know, and I cannot guess.

I have a feeling, however, that in his final days, his health destroyed, his mind tormented by doubts, his conscience far from clear, those chilling meetings with Eichmann would have been among his last thoughts before he died of cancer on 13 June 1946.

Perhaps that is why, despite his remarkable life, his will stipulated a simple funeral with no eulogies.

CHAPTER 15

A new nightmare

BY THE middle of December, the intensity of the Russian shelling of Budapest had increased dramatically. Dad used to sneak out and scrape snow off the balcony ledge for drinking water and watch what he called "the fireworks". In fact, not long before he died, he told me that one night, as he was crouching down on the snow-covered balcony, a bomb had exploded in a nearby building and the noise of it was so intense that he lost his hearing in one ear. This plagued him for the rest of his life.

By this time, Hungary was a vastly different country to the one that had existed before the Germans occupied it just eight months before. For a start, outside of the capital Budapest, the Nazis and their Hungarian collaborators had succeeded beyond Adolf Eichmann's wildest dreams: provincial Hungary was indeed *Judenrein* – 'cleansed of Jews'.

A total of 437,402 had already been transported from the rural regions, according to a jubilant Edmund Veesenmeyer, Hitler's representative in Hungary. Most of them had already been murdered in the gas chambers and ovens. Others were barely alive and still subject to unspeakable horrors; survivors recall "... living on bread and black, watery soup that had tufts of human hair in it, bones and mice ... and the grey, latherless soap made from human ashes." Tens of thousands of others were slave labourers in the Hungarian army.

The course of the war had also taken a sharp turn during that same period; the tide had turned very much in the Allies' favour. Their forces had landed in Normandy on 6 June 1944 – D-Day; Paris had been liberated in late August. By the beginning of October, the Red Army had beaten back the German *Wehrmacht* forces in the east and had entered Hungary. This panicked the German High Command, and on 14 October 1944, two Waffen SS divisions were sent to reinforce Budapest.

The Nazis removed the Hungarian prime minister and replaced him with Ferenc Szalazi, the head of the fascist Nyilas – the much-feared Arrow Cross party. Szalazi was a virulent anti-Semite whose rule only lasted 163 days, but during that time he was responsible for the deaths of tens of thousands of Jews. Regent Horthy was soon forced to abdicate and transported to captivity in Bavaria. For the 200,000 Jews still living in Budapest, a terrifying new nightmare was about to begin.

In the city, Jew and Gentile alike had already been suffering from the effects of the war: shelling, lack of power, food shortages, disease. Then there were the indiscriminate looting and acts of brutality, mainly against people wearing the yellow star.

At the behest of Veesenmeyer, thousands of Jewish men and women were also rounded up to be sent to Germany to work as slave labourers; and marched to the Austrian border where the SS then shipped many of them to labour camps in the Reich. Hundreds died along the way as the result of starvation or exposure to the cold.

The streets of downtown Budapest were a constant death trap for Jews thanks to marauding groups of drunken Arrow Cross men intent on robbery and murder. Taking evil to yet another level, these armed brutes would pluck Jews from their apartments or off the streets and march them to the edge of the Danube.

There they would be robbed, any gold teeth ripped out, and their shoes removed; then they would be tied together in threes, whereupon the fascist brutes, to save precious bullets, would shoot the heaviest person into the river and the body would drag the other two in. There are even grisly accounts of the Arrow Cross men using the latter as target practice.

This diabolical tactic was not confined to adults: on Christmas Eve the Arrow Cross attacked a Jewish orphanage and some of the children were taken to the Danube embankment and suffered the same fate. Little wonder then that during this period, this stretch of river was known as the 'Jewish Cemetery'.

In 2002, I stood at that same stretch of river and shed a tear at the thought of the estimated fifteen to twenty thousand men, women and children who died in this horrible way. I visualised the horror that happened there; imagining the faces of the children as they took off their shoes and turned to face the sneering faces of the gunman. Three years later, a unique memorial – *Shoes on the Danube Bank* – was erected on the side of the river in 2005 to commemorate these atrocities that mostly took place in December 1944 and January 1945; the monument features sixty pairs of shoes – men's, women's, and children's – sculpted in iron and set into the concrete embankment.

A Hungarian friend of mine, Peter Halas told me about his mother who was among the victims. She had gone to her parents' apartment to celebrate her own father's birthday. While there, Arrow Cross thugs burst into the building and took all the occupants, including Peter's mother and grandparents, to the riverbank and shot them. Luckily, my friend who was aged four at the time, had stayed at home because of a cold and thus missed the massacre.

All this helps explain why my parents hid in their overhead space – to avoid being snatched from their home or the street and murdered. Many Jews in Budapest did the same, hunkering down in basements, attics and other secret places as winter began to bite. How they managed to scrape together enough food to survive, I'll never know.

There are accounts of starving people sneaking out of shelters at night and butchering dead horses lying in the street. The animals at the zoo in Varosliget Park were also a food source: of the two thousand creatures at the start of the war, only fifteen survived. It's probable that my father would also have had to forage for scraps of food after dark, risking being shot by snipers or picked up by the fascists.

Meanwhile, the Soviet forces of up to a million men had advanced to within a few kilometres of Budapest. Much of the fighting had taken place around Lake Baloton, a popular holiday spot for Budapest residents, including my parents who used to vacation in a cabin there during the summer. It lies just over one hundred kilometres southwest of the city, about the same distance from my grandparents' home in Papa. My father used to say you could find the best *halaszle* (a traditional fish soup) in Hungary there.

The Germans continued to resist strongly. The Red Army artillery pounded the city every day. Nearly 33,000 German and 37,000 Hungarian soldiers, as well as more than 800,000 civilians, including the Jews, were essentially trapped like rats in a barrel. On 6 December, a defiant Hitler declared Budapest a "Festung", a fortress that would be "defended to the last man".

Corpses lay in the gutters and shop doorways; burnt-out cars blocked streets; buildings everywhere lay in ruins from the Russian bombardment. Walls were pockmarked with bullet holes. Power was intermittent. The atmosphere was full of dust and smoke and fear. Adolf Eichmann and his SS henchmen fled the city on 23 October, presumably in fear of their lives.

After the war, he was arrested by US authorities in Germany but escaped. He would next turn up in Argentina in 1960 when Israeli agents abducted him and took him back for trial in Jerusalem the following year. In the dock, Eichmann's breathtaking callousness was still on display: "The children have to be killed first," he said, "because where is the logic of killing a generation of older people and you leave alive a generation of possible avengers that create a race again."

Despite Eichmann's trite plea that he was 'only following orders', he was convicted of crimes against the Jewish people, crimes against humanity, war crimes, and membership in a criminal organization. He had never shown any remorse, once telling the Dutch journalist and Nazi collaborator Willem Sassen at his home in Argentina that he told his henchmen, "If it has to be, I told them, I will gladly jump into my grave in the knowledge that five million enemies of the Reich have already died like animals.'

Eichmann was sentenced to death on 15 December 1961. A few months later, on 1 June 1962, the infamous architect of the Final Solution was hanged. His body was cremated, and the ashes were spread at sea, beyond Israel's territorial waters.

Unfortunately, the proximity of the Russian forces did not deter the Arrow Cross; if anything, Szalazi and his cohorts simply stepped up their lethal pogrom against the remaining Jews. At the end of November, Arrow Cross hoodlums and Hungarian gendarmes began forcing them into the ghetto at Dohany Street.

This was effectively the last Jewish ghetto of the war to be set up and it consisted of six or seven blocks around the city's main synagogue – no more than a quarter-kilometre square. It was surrounded by brick walls and a high fence reinforced with planks; its four gates were guarded by uniformed police and armed Arrow-Cross men so that goods could not be sneaked in, and people could not get out.

It is appalling to note that, as the Jews were marched there, it was raining and cold, but the streets were lined with crowds of people, mainly women, who clapped as they went past, shouting abuse and revelling in their fate. These were not Nazis, just ordinary Hungarians. Beyond shameful.

Under the direction of the Jewish Council (in Stern's absence while in hiding, a new president had taken over), the ghetto was subdivided into ten districts with each one responsible for its food and fuel supplies. Communal kitchens were established and an internal police force, the 'gettorendeszet', was established.

Nearly 70,000 Budapest Jews, including nearly 6,000 children were moved into the ghetto at the height of a bitterly cold Budapest winter, an average of fourteen people per room. More than half that number had already been transported to Auschwitz. But the Nazis were in the process of dismantling the gas chambers and ovens at the death camp, and the transports had now ceased.

One observer, a Christian who visited the ghetto before it was completely sealed off gave this account:

> "Dirty water ran along the gutters, carrying with it garbage, dead rats, faeces and urine. The schools were closed so children roamed the streets. All the misery, poverty and suffering were out in the open, without shame or mercy. Among the crowds filling the street, there were people on old bicycles or with pushcarts, carrying old people who were unable to walk or sick people who were too weak to visit the nearest doctor's office. In every corner and doorway, there were people lying prostrated or curled up in the foetal position: some were homeless, others were dead, simply left to be picked up later by the collection brigades and buried in large pits in one of the parks."

The ghetto was only in existence for two months until the Russians arrived in January 1945, but still several thousands of its inhabitants died from a mix of hunger and cold and Arrow Cross brutality during that winter of 1944-1945. Heaps of corpses lay in the street, and a total of 2,281 bodies – many of them unidentifiable because they had been dead for weeks – were later buried in twenty-four common graves in the courtyard of the synagogue;

forty-five had been shot, including twenty-four women – probably by the Arrow Cross.

Today, one of those ubiquitous Raoul Wallenberg monuments graces the rear courtyard of the Great Synagogue which includes the awe-inspiring Memorial of the Hungarian Jewish Martyrs, that resembles a weeping willow whose leaves are inscribed with the names of victims. A fitting testament to the poor souls who died there.

The siege of Budapest by Russian and Romanian troops, often described as the bloodiest of the war after that of Stalingrad, lasted just fifty-one days from Boxing Day 1944 until February 13, 1945, when both German defenders and Hungarian authorities surrendered unconditionally. By then the so-called 'Leader of the Nation' Ferenc Szalasi had escaped, like Eichmann before him. He was later captured by US troops and brought back to Hungary; in 1946 he was tried and hanged for war crimes and crimes against humanity.

The battle for Budapest resulted in a huge human toll: according to noted Hungarian historian Krisztian Ungvari, more than 80,000 Soviet troops and 38,000 German and Hungarian soldiers were killed; about forty thousand civilians died, at least half of them Jews, many from starvation or disease. When the smoke cleared, eighty per cent of the capital's buildings were found to be damaged or destroyed, including historical landmarks such as the Hungarian Parliament building and Buda Castle; all five of Budapest's bridges across the Danube were destroyed.

This is an excerpt from a report by the Swiss Legation sent to the Ministry for Foreign Affairs in Bern towards the end of March 1945:

"Half the city at a rough estimate is in ruins. Certain

quarters have, according to the Soviet forces, suffered more than Stalingrad. The quays along the Danube, and in particular the Erzsebet (Elizabeth) Bridge and the Chain Bridge, are utterly destroyed. On Palace Hill, there is practically nothing left standing. The Royal Palace has been burnt to the ground. The Coronation Church has collapsed. The Parliament Buildings are badly damaged, though their facade is still intact. The Ritz, Hungaria, Carlton, Vadaszkürt and Gellert Hotels are in ruins. Part of the Bank Buildings and the National Casino have been destroyed by fire."

The hand-to-hand fighting was ferocious. Weary and half-starved combatants on both sides, fuelled by hatred and fear, brawled and battled street to street, block by block, building to building, above and below ground, using whatever weapons they could lay their hands on – flamethrowers, grenades, machine guns, and often bayonets; neither side showed any mercy to the other, nor to any civilian unlucky enough to be caught in the middle. They were equally vulnerable to the Russian planes that circled above the ruined rooftops, strafed the streets with bullets, and dropped small bombs on anything that moved.

Grotesquely, amid the soul-sapping chaos and confusion of the increasingly bloody battle, the Germans and the Arrow Cross still managed to find the energy to hatch an insane plan to burn down the Jewish ghetto and annihilate all its inhabitants. Thanks to the actions of Raoul Wallenberg and other foreign diplomats, the plan was aborted. Reports suggest that Wallenberg told the German army commander that he would be held personally responsible for the massacre and hanged as a war criminal after hostilities ended. On 18 January 1944, the Soviet Red Army liberated the ghetto and found three thousand dead bodies; these were then buried in the courtyard of the Great Synagogue.

Over the next few weeks, the urban warfare continued in the

city streets and residential suburbs, until finally, on February 13, Budapest was 'liberated' as the Russians would have it. That same day, the surviving inhabitants who had been in hiding for months – including my parents, Laszlo and Erzsebet Kalmar – emerged, disoriented and disbelieving, on to the chaotic, snow-covered streets and whatever remained of the beleaguered city.

CHAPTER 16

The search for 'Zsuzsiki'

THAT HISTORIC moment of 'liberation' (I put quote marks around the word with a sense of irony because Hungary, far from being given freedom by the Russians, would now face further oppression and subjugation under them) arrived just eleven months since the Nazis occupied Hungary in March 1944 and the nightmare for Jews began; the Soviets would occupy the country for another forty-seven years until they left in 1991.

All these years later, I can't begin to imagine my parents' feelings as they stood, arms around each other, outside their apartment for the first time in months. Or, for that matter, the scenes of apocalyptic devastation that they would have witnessed all around them through the cloying dust, fumes and smoke.

A thousand questions would have clouded their minds: was the maids' family in the countryside taking good care of me? Was I in good health? Did I have enough to eat? In the middle of a war zone, how would they find me? Mum always told me that their immediate priority was to go and pick me up. They were desperate to see me and hold me in their arms.

I still marvel at how they survived, cooped up in that cold, cramped, candle-lit space as Christmas came and went, constantly worried about what would become of me, and terrified that a shell would hit their building and end their hopes and dreams. It must have been an unbelievably tortuous time and I truly believe that the shocking stress must have affected my mother's heart and contributed to the first of two strokes thirty years later.

But their euphoria at the liberation didn't last long: amid the shocking silence that had enveloped the city for the first time in months as the bombardment had ceased, my parents were hit by a new, unbelievable bombshell. The two maids, Borbola and Zsofia arrived at the Deak Ferenc Street apartment with shocking news: they had been unable to reach the place where their relatives lived in the northern part of the country because of intense fighting between the German and Russian forces in the region.

'My God, so where is Zsuzsiki (a pet name for me that my mother used all her life)?!' my mother cried. "What have you done with my baby?" A tearful Borbola had then explained that, with Russian forces everywhere and tanks and artillery causing destruction in the city and surrounding countryside, they had felt it was too dangerous to bring me back to Budapest so … they'd left me in a Jewish orphanage in Miskolc for safekeeping! And besides, Borbola said sheepishly, they had expected the worst – that their employers had been captured or killed by then.

Utterly horrified by this new twist, mum and dad immediately decided to go and fetch me. Nothing else mattered. But, of course, it wasn't that simple. Even with the Nazis suddenly gone like a wisp of smoke in a sandstorm, danger lurked everywhere. For a start, the Russians had begun as the Germans began – looting buildings, robbing men and raping women and girls.

Estimates of the number of victims of the Soviet sexual violence in Budapest range from 5,000 to 50,000. Mothers were raped by drunken soldiers in front of their children and husbands. Girls as young as twelve were dragged from their fathers and raped in succession by ten to fifteen soldiers and often infected with venereal disease. The Red Army even had a twisted euphemism for this systemic sexual brutality: 'peeling potatoes.'

I still have flashbacks to an incident that happened not long before my third birthday when I witnessed a Russian soldier attack a woman in the courtyard behind our building; her screams continue to haunt me. So, no woman or girl was safe from the predatory, vengeful soldiers, even if she was in the company of a male. Many would try to make themselves as old and ugly as possible when venturing out. My father liked to say, with a certain amount of glee, how he 'dirtied up' my mum to make her look unattractive before they set off to find me.

It is a matter of historical record that the Soviet soldiers looted, robbed, stole everything that could be moved, and they destroyed on site what could not be dismantled; they robbed the machinery of entire factories, tore wristwatches and wedding rings off men, earrings and necklaces off women, and even the boots off the feet of fallen Hungarian soldiers. They threw furniture, art objects, paintings, and carpets out of windows onto the pavements. Then Russian freight cars hauled the collected wealth of Hungary out of the country, much as the Nazis had transported Jewish assets over the previous twelve months.

Copying another page from the Nazi playbook, the Russians also forced thousands of men into labour gangs to help with reconstruction. So, for many of the city's surviving 100,000 Jews (out of an original total of 200,000), it was a case of jumping from the frying pan into the fire. But at least their victory over the German forces gave my mum and dad the opportunity to escape the dark, cramped space and walk outside in the fresh air. They had escaped the Nazis, the Arrow Cross, deportation and the death camps, but the question now was – could they survive the Soviet soldiers as they rampaged around Budapest? And more to the point, how could they leave the city and reach Miskolc? Travelling through what was still a war zone would be a nightmare.

But mum and dad did not have to think twice – they were more scared of losing their child than of facing Russian soldiers; my father's first move was to contact an acquaintance, Emery Fouest, who happened to be the head of the anti-Nazi movement in Hungary and therefore had good relations with the Russians;

fortunately, Fouest was able to obtain the necessary documents that would allow my parents to travel north.

In the middle of what was one of the coldest winters in decades, they then set off *on foot* to find me – there were no trams or taxis running in the city to take them to a railway station because of the debris and burnt-out vehicles in the shambolic streets. Dead bodies hung from lampposts with placards proclaiming their alleged 'crimes'. Both mum and dad must have been bone-weary and starving after months of self-imposed captivity, but they were determined to find the orphanage where the maids left me.

They lucked out on their first day in the outskirts of the city when a farmer took pity on them and gave them a lift on his horse and open cart to a railway station in the small town of Godollo, about thirty kilometres northeast of Budapest; snow had begun to fall again and they were overjoyed to be able to buy hot soup and bread at the station; it was their first hot meal in weeks, and they smiled at each other as they wolfed down the food.

The following day there were rattletrap cattle trains running and they boarded one that was heading north. Years later, dad used to laugh when he told the story about the old, clapped-out locomotive that kept running out of fuel; the passengers, he said, would have to get off and rip up the sleepers on other snow-covered tracks to stoke the engine fire and get them moving again. On the third day, they caught a goods train to Miskolc that had a decent supply of coal.

Then something happened that my mother for the rest of her life described as "an absolute miracle": an old lady sitting opposite them started chatting amiably to them; she said she was surprised to see a Jewish couple in the area as most had been deported. "Why are you going to Miskolc?" she asked. My mother cried as she explained what had happened to them in Budapest and told the woman that they were trying to find their daughter who had been left in an orphanage near Miskolc. The old lady asked them to describe her. "She's red-headed," mum said, "and she's got a brown sweater with her name, 'Zsuzsanna', embroidered on it in beige."

According to my mum, the old woman looked thoroughly taken aback. but then she clapped her hands together and said: "But I know someone who has taken in a red-headed girl wearing a sweater just like the one you talk of!"

Imagine my parents' joy on hearing this news. Neither of my parents were religious but, ever after, they described randomly meeting this woman as an 'act of God', and that, somehow, I was blessed. And when they arrived in Miskolc, they found that, sure enough, the orphanage had been bombed and then evacuated with the children being fostered out to families in the surrounding area. Including me.

It turned out that, in the short time since the orphanage had closed, I had been fostered by six different families – a case of 'pass-the-parcel' over concerns about taking in a Jewish child. After a while, each of the host families would get the jitters and hand me on to someone else.

When they arrived at the village mentioned by the woman on the train, finally, joyfully, they found me living with an old lady on a farm. She had kept me hidden in a barn where I slept in a wooden tub with the feed for the cattle. When I was a self-conscious teenager, my mother used to take great delight in telling me that, when they first clapped eyes on me in that country barn, most of my beautiful red hair had fallen out and I was covered in lice and dirt, scabs and sores.

Of course, I don't remember a thing about that time, but many decades later when I visited a petting farm with my goddaughter, I became quite disturbed while watching her milk a cow; the smell seemed eerily familiar and gave me goosebumps. I can only assume it had something to do with the time I spent in that cold barn – a deep-buried sensory snapshot that was filed in my memory.

That brown and beige sweater survived for many years

afterwards as a sort of family talisman, a tangible and emotional reminder that I had again escaped death before being reunited with my anxious parents. I even had a similar one made that I use as a prop for my presentation to schools and community centres.

Before returning to Budapest, my mum and dad rented a room in the village for a few days to recover their strength and spirit and give me plenty of baths! As for the farm lady who had cared for me – 'Aunt Juliska', as we called her – for many years after, my mum and dad would regularly bring her to the capital city as a reward for keeping me safe.

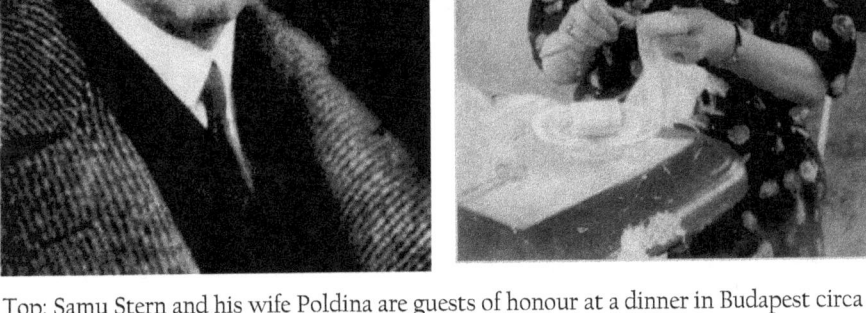

Top: Samu Stern and his wife Poldina are guests of honour at a dinner in Budapest circa 1938.
Above left: Stern in 1943, the year before the Nazi's arrived in Budapest.
Above right: Poldina Stern at her favourite pastime – needlework.

Top: The 1937 Grand Assembly of the Pest Israelite Congregation at their headquarters in 12 Sip Street, Budapest. Samu Stern, president of the Jewish community, is seated on the speaker's left.

Above: The Stern family gravestone. The names of Rozsi and her husband Gyorgy Bamberger are inscribed on the left-hand side, while the centre inscription says: 'Stern Samune Reisz Leopoldina 1870-1937. Stern Samu 1874 - 1946.'

Right: The cover of Samu Stern's book *Race Against Time*, dictated to a secretary just before he died in 1946.

Above: Samu Stern's granddaughter Lidia Bamberger and her family in Budapest in 1961 – husband Pal Sas, and sons Istvan and Peter (left). Peter's daughter Anna helped us with our research for this book.

Right: Lidia was 19 when she and her parents, Rozsi and Gyorgy Bamberger, embarked on the Kasztner Train on 30 June 1944 and escaped to Switzerland.

Above: The map shows all the regional Hungarian ghettoes created by Adolf Eichmann and his henchmen in 1944. These contained more than 430,000 Jewish men, women and children who were then transported to Auschwitz between 15 May and 9 July 1944. Papa, where my mother and I were locked up, can be seen to the west of Budapest.

Right: the copy of the Papa ghetto deportation list with the names of my mother, my grandparents and myself. This was given to me by Yad Vashem in Jerusalem.

HEROES AND VILLAINS
Top row: Rudolph Kasztner, Raoul Wallenberg, Hannah Szenes.
Middle row: Adolf Eichmann, Ferenc Szalasi, Miklos Horthy.
Bottom row: Hermann Krumey, Dieter Wisliceny, Edmund Veesenmeyer.

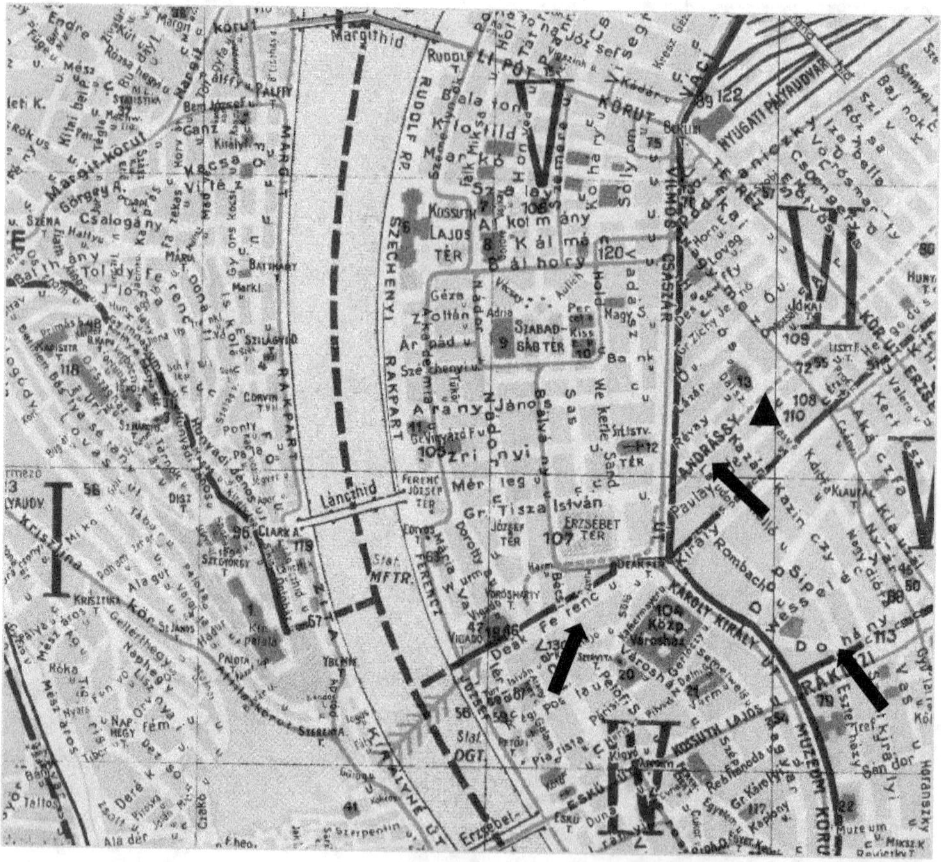

Above: A map depicting Budapest just before the 1939-1945 war. The black arrows point to Deak Ferenc Street where we lived until we fled to Austria in 1948, Andrassy Avenue and Dohany Street where the city's Grand Synagogue was located and, in 1944, the Budapest ghetto.

Right: Esku Street where the Stern family lived next to the Pest side entrance to Elizabeth Bridge. The street no longer exists.

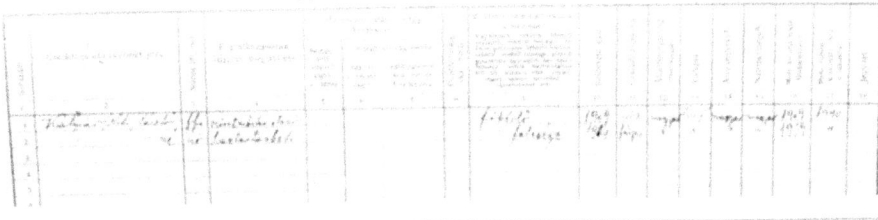

Top: The record of my father's labour battalion conscription.

Other photos: An estimated 42,000 Jewish conscripts died while working in Hungarian slave labour units.

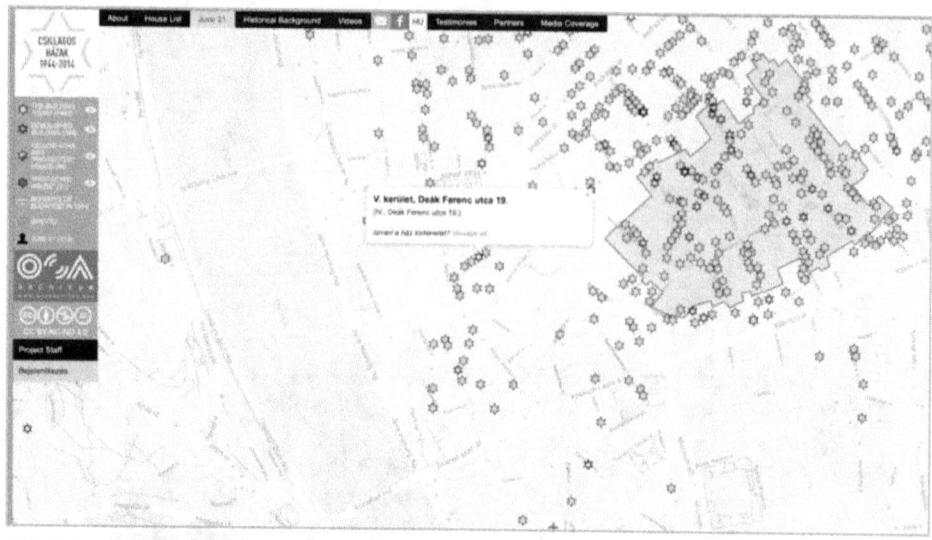

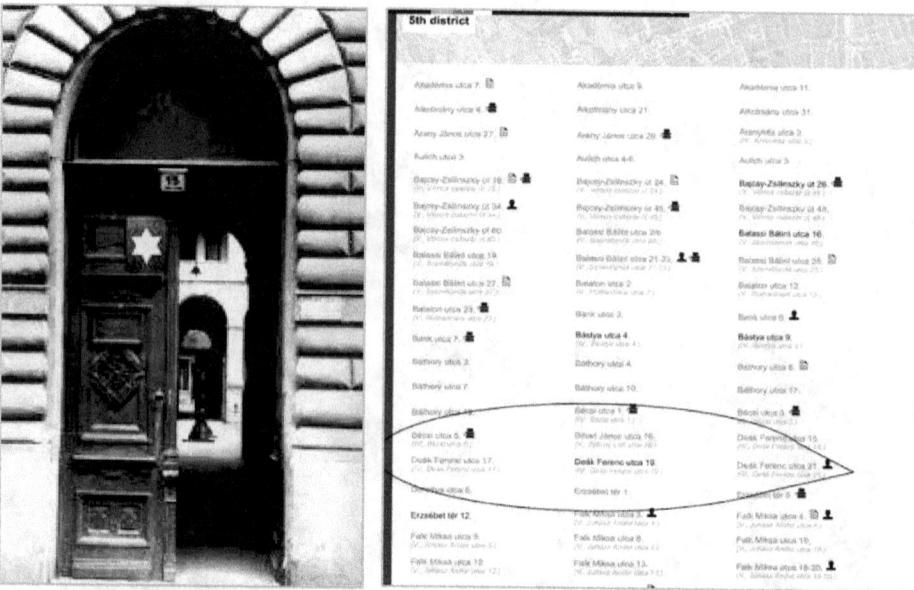

Top: There is a useful interactive website that shows each of the 'yellow star' houses in Budapest in 1944: www.yellowstarhouses.org.

Above: One of the city's designated houses.

Right: Our old apartment is listed on the site as a yellow star location.

Above: The 'Shoes on the Danube' monument erected in April 2005.

Right: Arrow Cross 'Greenshirt' thugs execute Jews along the bank of the Danube River in 1944. Estimates suggest that 20,000 died in this way.

Bottom: The Holocaust memorial plaque honouring the victims massacred by the fascist Arrow Cross party on the east bank of the river.

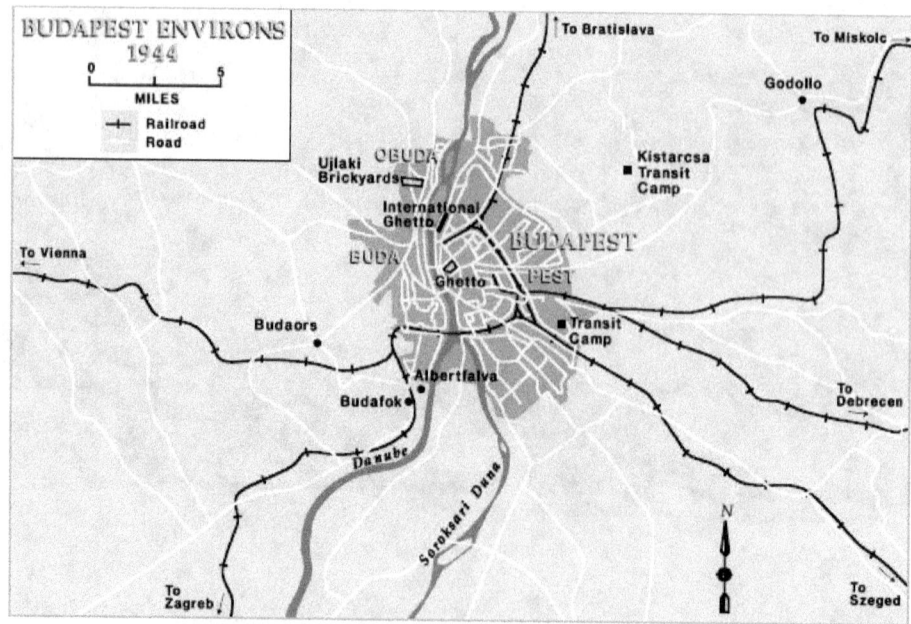

These maps show the locations of many crucial Hungarian Holocaust sites in 1944. They include: the Ujlaki brickyards where the Nazis concentrated more than 70,000 Jews before marching them to camps in Austria; the two Budapest ghettoes; the Dohany Street synagogue; the Gestapo HQ; and the Swedish embassy annex where Raoul Wallenberg worked tirelessly to save Jews.

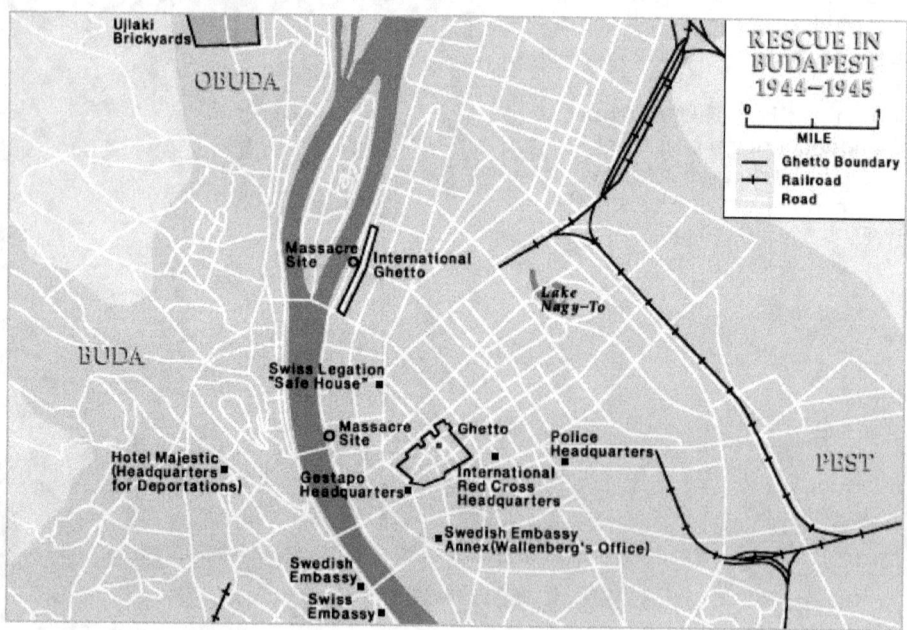

Top: Zsa Zsa Gabor, the Hungarian actress.

Middle: A poster for a popular film in the 1930s.

Bottom: Budapest fashion in 1938.

Top: Vilmos Csaszar Street, Budapest in 1938. My father's textile shop was located there.

Above: Szechenyi Baths in 1940. As Budapest's Jews faced mounting levels of oppression, the city's other residents continued to enjoy a carefree existence.

SCENES FROM A SIEGE

Top: Victorious Red Army soldiers enter Budapest following a fifty-day siege of the city.

Above middle: Each of Budapest's five bridges was destroyed by the retreating Germans.

Above: A Russian soldier amid the city's ruins.

Right: An aeroplane crashed into an apartment block during the siege.

Top: Jews from rural areas of Hungary undergoing selection on arrival at Auschwitz-Birkenau. Most would be sent immediately to the gas chambers.

Middle: Hungarian Jews, mostly women and children, leaving the cattle trucks which had taken them to Auschwitz and almost certainly to their deaths.

Bottom: A Hungarian gendarme stands guard as Jews are rounded up in Budapest in October 1944, watched by jeering crowds.

PART THREE

1945 – Present

"We cannot understand fascism, but we can and must understand from where it springs, and we must be on our guard ... because what happened can happen again. For this reason, it is everyone's duty to reflect on what happened."

Primo Levi, noted Italian writer and Auschwitz survivor

CHAPTER 17

Saved from the secret police

ACCORDING TO my parents, life under the Soviet regime was somewhat better than it had been under the Nazis but far from the proletarian paradise promised by the communists. As my father once told me, Hungary simply swapped one form of state-sponsored/ oppression for another. German Tiger tanks were replaced by Russian Tsyganovs and one brutal secret police regime succeeded another. The Soviet-inspired Hungarian secret police, the 'State Protection Authority', (known as the AVH) simply took over the Gestapo police headquarters at Number 60 Andrassy Avenue. In other words, the fascists and the communists might have a differing ideology, but they shared the same mindless methodology of torture, terror and sham trials.

The same applied to forced labour – like the Nazis before them, the Russians conscripted tens of thousands of Jews and Gentiles alike to work as slave labour on reconstruction projects in Hungary while others were deported to Soviet gulags. 'Meet the new boss, same as the old boss', as a 1970s song lyric puts it nicely.

Yet, notionally at least, the Jews were safer under the Soviets, but only marginally so. Stalin, at least, did not fashion his own version of the Final Solution. You could say he was a believer in equal opportunities: his men did not discriminate over who they would arrest, brutalise or kill. *Anyone* considered an enemy of the state – petty criminals, political dissidents and non-conformists alike would find themselves in the basement at Andrassy howling for mercy. And it soon became clear to everyone that the Russians were not just 'liberators', they were occupiers.

Years later, my dad father talked about the Russian soldiers who he described as 'very primitive farm boys'. He said they were fascinated by wrist watches which they had not seen before. "The soldiers stole them from Hungarians, but they didn't know they had to be wound up, and when they stopped, they simply grabbed another one," he said to me once. My father also told me that one time, when the soldiers had burst into our apartment, they danced on his precious records, breaking them all.

Although I would only have been three or four years old at this time, I can remember some random things – for example, the maids reading stories to me in the kitchen including one about a boy called Donny who was made of cork. And vague, blurry images of our apartment still lurk in my memory banks: it had folding doors that opened three rooms into one, with a grand piano in the front room that my mother loved to play. I also have a clear memory of our last Christmas in that apartment: there was a beautiful tree decorated with sugared lollies (which I loved!), and one of the toys underneath (that I opened) was a large Mickey Mouse soft toy dressed as a cowboy.

Even when the Third Reich surrendered unconditionally to the Allies and the Russians in early May 1945, any thoughts that Red Army would leave Hungary to manage its own affairs again were dispelled slowly but surely. It took until 1949 for the People's Republic of Hungary to come fully into being. But, in the intervening period, the Soviet military gradually replaced the freely elected government with the Hungarian Communist Party, and nationalised the economy; this, inevitably, produced economic stagnation, lower standards of living and a creeping sense of despair amongst the Magyar population.

The Stalinists were, of course, obsessed with secrecy and security, and had agents and informers everywhere, even in the schools.

Kids were asked to spy on their parents: I remember being given forms at school for me to fill in details about their lives – what newspapers they read, what radio stations they listened to, or if they said bad things about the communist party.

Yet, for mum and dad, however, it must still have been a stunning relief to come down from their dark crawl space and live like human beings in the light again; they no longer had to be constantly alert to Arrow Cross footsteps on the stairway, or fearful of being deported to a probable death. I know dad would have been overjoyed to hear on the radio towards the end of January that Soviet troops had liberated Auschwitz-Birkenau.

My mother must have been desperate to hear news of my grandparents who had been sent there almost a year before; had they survived? Would they be arriving back soon? It was a lingering form of torture from the Nazi era. Mum would have thought about them every day and prayed for them at least as often. It wasn't until late 1947 that a family friend who'd been in Auschwitz told her that she had witnessed Jeno and Irma going to the gas chambers straight after the train had arrived. Knowing how much my mother loved her parents, she would have been utterly heartbroken by that. I'm certain that a pang of guilt remained with her all her remaining days for, as she saw it, abandoning them. That, despite the fact that they forcefully insisted she save herself and her baby. Otherwise, we would have suffered the same fate.

Along with the Nazis, many of the previous anti-Jewish decrees and regulation were swept away by the Soviets, and the Jews were able to return to their professions and open their businesses again, albeit subject to the communist way of doing things – ie strong state intervention. The Jewish community was merely subjected to the same anti-religious and anti-bourgeois measures as followers of other faiths. Many Jews joined the communist party, believing it would create a society where there would be no 'Jewish problem' or anti-Semitism.

My father did not care too much about any of this; he was just eager to get back to work. He was also the sort of practical, pragmatic person who was confident, given a chance, that he could 'work the system' – any system. And, indeed, he quickly started up a new textile business in the city which must have been successful because we soon moved to a bigger apartment across the river in Buda.

He liked to tell people with a smile that the seed money for his new business came from the book business. Here's why: on the way back from rescuing me in the country, he met this man who had several hundred Russian/Hungarian dictionaries; dad bought them all for a song and then sold them for twenty times what he paid for them when we got back to Budapest. He also had hidden some bales of cloth in the cellar of our building at the time of the German occupation, and these two factors enabled him to get back on his feet.

I must have inherited my father's entrepreneurial genes because there was a family legend that he often recounted when we had moved to Australia. This is how it went: "Suzi disappeared from the shop one day, and when we heard a commotion outside, Erzsebet and I ran out to find a crowd had gathered around her while she sold them wrapping paper in exchange for oranges and chocolates!" The brown paper had been used to cover the bales of cloth and I had obviously seen an opportunity to recycle it!

While he worked hard to make this new enterprise succeed, my father also dreamed of taking us all to the United States. But my mother resisted his attempts to persuade her to leave until the moment she learnt that her parents had been murdered.

By 1948, three years after the Nazis had been sent packing, his business was prospering, and he believed with all his heart that he could do similarly well in the US, given the chance. He applied for American visas for the three of us, and this inadvertently set in motion the chain of events that led us to flee our home and our country. By now, the communists had effective control of the government and they called him into the trade ministry to discuss his visa application. He was apprehensive but they were all smiles. "We like what you have been doing," they told him. "Perhaps you could be our textile industry representative in America."

Initially, my father could not believe his luck. This, after all, had been his dream. But there was a catch: mum and I must remain in Hungary as human collateral to stop us all defecting. Dad immediately and emphatically turned down the offer. The communists were not impressed, and suddenly, after two years of post-Nazi relative freedom from threats and unpleasantness, a dark cloud now hovered over us again. When he returned home from this meeting, my father knew he had screwed up badly: "They now think of me as an enemy of the state," he told mum. "Now I'm a marked man."

Shattered by this turn of events, and well aware what had happened to others who had fallen foul of the communists, dad started feverishly looking for a means to escape. He had been hoping against hope to hear that his US visa application had been successful but then, a couple of days later, a friend of his who worked for the AVO, the secret police, phoned him: "My colleagues are coming to arrest you on Monday," he said.

That was just three days away. If they followed their standard procedure, they would arrive during the night, break down the door to our apartment and then drag my father down to a sinister black Pobjeda (Victory) car, its engine idling on the street below. The AVH sadists were notorious for inhumane physical and psychological coercion in those dank cellars; their menu of torture included electric shocks, beatings, fingernail removal, starvation, and sleep deprivation. Hangings were common.

In desperation, my father asked around friends and acquaintances for ways he could get the three of us out of the country, knowing that any one of them could betray him. But then one of his rowing mates told him about this young Russian soldier who delivered mail between Budapest and Vienna – 250km apart – but who was also rumoured to be smuggling people out of Hungary for a price.

Dad was prepared to pay anything to save his family from falling into the hands of the secret police. And so, on the day after, Saturday, he closed the business in the late afternoon while mum packed a small suitcase and said farewell to our home. Later that night, in a dark lane, we met up with two other couples, and the Russian soldier who ordered his passengers to lie down on the floor of a small van while he stacked bags of mail on top of us. I can vividly remember that dark, dangerous night. Sometimes, I even dream about it ...

July 1948. It was around 2am. A warm, dry windless night. The old Russian truck rocked and rattled as we sped along a quiet road on the south side of the Danube. It was an olive-green flat-bed with wooden footboards, a canvas top and an opening at the rear. A faded red star adorned each of the two doors.

I was nearly six years old, and we were headed for the Austrian border ... away from our old life and the people who wanted to destroy us. Scared rigid by the tense drama that was playing out, I lay on the floor in the back of the vehicle among large mailbags gazing up at dark clouds flitting across the moon in a velvet sky.

A musty smell pervaded the cramped space – a nose-wrinkling mix of damp sacking and automotive oil and human fear. Inside, all that I could make out were the pale faces and wide eyes of the other passengers, as they shivered with repressed fear. Outside, the dark landscape looked unscathed by the recent war, unlike the battered city we had left behind.

It had been nearly three hours since we'd left Budapest with another two couples, strangers who were also fleeing the communist regime. I never knew their names or why they were also taking such a colossal risk. And I never saw them again after that fateful night. But it was clear that *we* had no choice – my father, Laszlo Kalmar, was deemed by the Russians to be an enemy of the state whose fate was likely to be a lonely death at the hands of the secret police, or a pitiful existence in the salt mines of Siberia.

Our driver was a Russian soldier whose job it was to deliver mail between Red Army depots in Hungary and Austria, but sometimes he risked his life smuggling refugees across the border. Not for altruistic reasons, of course, he was just in it for the money.

Suddenly, I felt the Red Army truck begin to slow before it screeched to a halt, its engine ticking noisily in the sudden stillness. I became aware of lights and strange sounds. *The border crossing!* The tension in the back of the vehicle was palpable. My mother held a scarf over my mouth to stop me from crying out while my father's worried eyes tried to feign reassurance. I clutched my doll more tightly – it was a boy doll, like a ventriloquist's dummy with dimpled cheeks, black and white checked pants and a green tie. Other than one small suitcase, it was all that we had with us. Then my nostrils flared as the sudden, coarse smell of cheap cigarettes wafted into the back of the truck in the warm breeze.

Dogs barked, then I heard human voices – Russian voices, heavy, guttural, similar to those I'd heard in the streets of burnt-out Budapest. My mother's hand tightened around mine. My father looked at me, his brow furrowed, and put a finger to his lips. I had no idea what the strange voices were saying, but I recognised one of them as our driver's. But he was laughing, and the exchange seemed cordial. Maybe money changed hands. Either way, there was no attempt to search the back of the truck. That was a miracle because we heard later that, on another trip, the soldier and his human cargo had been shot dead at the Austrian border.

But that night, thankfully, I heard an abrupt double-thump on the truck bonnet and then the engine revved up, there was a loud grinding noise as the ancient clutch engaged. Suddenly, the truck lurched forward, and we were on our way. I saw my parents smile wanly at each other, and broad grins crease the other couples' faces.

Against all the odds, we'd survived.

Postscript: two AVO thugs arrived early on the following Monday morning at the apartment just as my father's friend had warned where they found our maid Borbola down on her knees praying for us. Frustrated by our escape, they took her into custody. She was later released without charge and, I am relieved to say, without torture.

CHAPTER 18

Goodnight Vienna

WHEN WE arrived in Austria's capital at the end of July 1948, after our nightmare journey in the back of the mail van, we were all exhausted, scared and virtually penniless. The latter fact only became apparent to my father when, the day after our arrival, he went to a money exchange and found that his stash of Hungarian currency had become next to worthless.

Two years previously, in 1946, the Hungarian pengo had been replaced by the florint as hyperinflation wreaked havoc on the Magyar economy. A Soviet-style 'Three-Year Plan' started in August 1947, and more than 90 percent of the economy was nationalized including the banks. Then, in 1948, the Budapest Stock and Commodity Exchange was shut down and its assets taken into state hands. The value of the florint in foreign exchange markets dived ... and suddenly, we were broke.

Dad had some American dollars that kept us going for a bit, along with the few valuables we'd been able to bring with us. (As a side note, twenty years later when the stock exchange was re-started, it was relocated to Deak Ferenc Street – the same street we used to live in.) Because we were 'illegals', he could not get a proper job. Instead, he eked out what little we had by playing bridge for money in the city's classic coffee houses that resembled those he'd frequented back in Budapest before the German occupation.

Our cash problems worsened when my mother's diamond ring was stolen from the room we were renting from a widow in Vienna while we were having a bath. Because we were 'illegal' my parents were frightened to go the police, but they always suspected the landlady.

Vienna – birthplace of Johann Strauss, Marie Antoinette and Amon Goeth (the psychopathic death camp commandant featured in Schindler's List) – was still under the control of four victorious Allied powers – the US, UK, France and Russia, and subdivided into four separate occupation zones governed by one of the respective powers. But the historical central area of the capital city was designated as an international zone and control of it changed between the Allies every month. Like Budapest, the city had been on its knees financially at the end of the war but, in 1948, a massive injection of aid came via the US-inspired Marshall Plan, and Austria's recovery began in real earnest.

My memories of our time in Vienna are pretty sketchy as I was only six years old but, looking back after more than seven decades, I still remember the streets being crowded with eager shoppers and stylish ladies, the restaurants being open and the shop windows full of Vienna's trademark confectionary (although a photograph from *Life* magazine from that time shows passers-by stopping to look longingly at a display of pastries and *sachertorte* – but clearly unable to buy them).

I also recall a lot of building work going on around the city centre to replace or renovate buildings battered during the war, including the fire-damaged St Stephen's Cathedral; bombed-out ruins and bullet-pocked walls were also still very much in evidence – indeed, there were a number of female work gangs known as 'trummerfrauen' – debris women, tasked with removing the massive amounts of rubble. Many of these ladies were widows with small children who worked in return for meagre cash payments and ration cards.

That same period marked the beginning of the Cold War, as the western powers vied with Russia for control and influence in Europe. From the noirish films of the time set in Vienna like

Graham Greene's *The Third Man*, it's clear that there was a great deal of smuggling, spying and skulduggery going on to which, of course, I was completely oblivious. However, even at that young age I was aware of a dark side to the city and, despite the uptick in the city's economy, a lot of poverty – beggars in the alleys and scrawny, scruffy children in raggedy clothing everywhere, many of them probably orphaned refugees cast adrift in the chaos of post-war Europe. It's possible that they came from the several overcrowded Displaced Persons' camps in and around Vienna, many of whose inhabitants were Jewish Holocaust survivors.

One awe-inspiring moment from my brief time in Vienna that I remember clearly came when my parents gave me a special treat by taking me to the Prater amusement park in Leopoldstat, one of the city's main tourist districts and I first clapped eyes on the 'wiener riesenrad' or giant Ferris wheel which was 260 metres tall.

Austria's capital was, and still is, a German-speaking city and my mother told me that I seemed to pick up the guttural language more quickly than her or my dad; ironically, we had previously only heard German being used by Nazi soldiers barking orders in Papa and Budapest. Consequently, I became the de facto interpreter, helping my mother negotiate with shopkeepers and tram conductors and the like. I also seemed to have a better sense of direction than her, as we navigated the unfamiliar streets and avenues.

Mum also decided to use our time in Vienna to provide me with some cultural education by taking me to places of interest, including the city's fascinating museums. One lesson I learnt very quickly (and painfully) from her was to curb my natural energy and enthusiasm – this came after a visit to a museum where, despite her warning to slow down, I was rushing up the high side of the stairway, only to fall and fracture my arm!

Our little family hunkered down in Vienna for several months while my parents worked out what we were going to do next now that we were safe from the Russians. Australia wasn't the first choice – my parents told me years later that they had thought it wasn't a civilised place! In fact, my father had initially pursued his ambition to take us all to the United States and he spent long hours filling in forms and lobbying the US State Department and the Jewish Refugee Board. But his heart sank when he was told there was already a long queue of people with similar aspirations ahead of us; he concluded that we needed a Plan B if we were to get away from Europe any time soon.

By then, Australia had revealed that they were willing to accept non-European migrants; hitherto Europe, and predominantly Great Britain, had been the source of the vast majority of immigrants under the controversial 'White Australia' policy. The Australian government had even set up a new Department of Immigration in 1945, with the new minister, Arthur Caldwell declaring: "We must populate, or we will perish. We must fill this country, or we will lose it. We need to protect ourselves against the yellow peril from the north. Our current population of 7,391,000 (about one person per square mile) leaves a land as vast as Australia, under-protected."

In those days, of course, the "yellow peril" Caldwell rather politically incorrectly referred to was not China but Japan which, after its infamous assault on Pearl Harbour in 1941, had considered invading Australia. It had also attacked Darwin and Sydney Harbour. The Australian government thought that a major increase in population would be the solution to the nation's future security against future aggression. Caldwell hoped it would eventually reach twenty million by the end of the twentieth century, and he got his wish – seventy-five years later, it stands at more than twenty-five million.

In 1948, the same year we took refuge in Vienna, Australia introduced a new Nationality and Citizenship Act that created the status of 'Australian citizen' for the first time (a few years later, this was the vehicle that enabled us to become full Australian citizens). Incredibly, prior to then, Australians, even those born there, could only hold the status of British subjects. Indeed, the first citizenship ceremony was held at Albert Hall in Canberra in 1949.

"We want, and will welcome, new healthy citizens who are determined to become good Australians." That was Arthur Caldwell again. It was enough for dad to act. He decided that the American dream was a busted flush and contacted a female relative who had left Hungary several years previously to emigrate Down Under; according to dad, he had helped her pack a container with her belongings. I remember him telling me how they had hollowed out the legs of her chairs and sofas and filled the spaces with diamonds and gold jewellery. Happily, this woman agreed to pay for our passage and my parents set about arranging passage to the 'Lucky Country'.

By now, mum who had suffered depression due to our frugal circumstances in Vienna, was saying that Australia was beginning to sound like paradise. And, compared to the hatred and the hell they'd experienced in the previous few years, that's exactly what it proved to be.

CHAPTER 19

Viva Vivaldi

IN THAT post-war, mid-century era, travel from Europe to Australia was mostly by sea. The main servicer of that route was an Italian shipping line based in Genoa: *Lloyd Triestino* had three vessels sailing to Freemantle, Melbourne and Sydney from the Mediterranean. One of those ships was the *Ugolino Vivaldi*, named after a thirteenth century explorer who went missing while trying to reach India by circumnavigating west around Africa. Not necessarily a good omen!

The *Ugolini Vivaldi* had been built in 1945 and spent the first few years of its life plying routes around South America as a cargo ship before being refitted to take passengers and reassigned to the Australia route in 1949. It was 150m long with a nineteen-metre beam and weighed nearly nine thousand tonnes with a cruising speed of fifteen knots; it accommodated ninety-five people in first class and seven hundred and thirty-five in third class, mainly in dormitories housed in the former cargo holds. According to shipping records, the *UV* only made ten return trips from Genoa to Australia from 1949 to 1951 before it was reassigned to another route.

To reach Genoa, we went on an aeroplane for the first time in early April 1949; that was a big thing for a little girl in those days and naturally I was both nervous and excited. Sadly, it turned out to be an unhappy experience as the aircraft was buffeted by strong winds as we crossed the Alps and I felt sick.

Nowadays, I wonder what my parents thought as they took this momentous flight – the first step in a long journey to a new life on the other side of the world. Excited, of course, and apprehensive, but no doubt hopeful of putting all the horrors behind them and making a fresh start. Dad, I know, would have been feeling confident that he could make a 'red hot go' of whatever lay ahead of him in Australia.

Newly arrived in Genoa, we briefly stayed with a very stylish blonde lady in Genoa until the actual day of sailing; she was either a family friend or an old girlfriend of my father's. To be honest, I don't remember much about the external look of the *Ugolino Vivaldi* because, once on it, you lost all perspective. But I remember there seemed plenty of deck space to run around. Photographs taken in its heyday show it to be quite a sleek, handsome vessel, with a pale yellow and blue funnel, marred only by tall, ugly derricks erected on its main deck for loading and unloading cargo or supplies.

As a six-year-old, I was quite oblivious to the pivotal moment that was about to change my entire life – we were leaving Europe and its wearisome post-war disruption for a new life in a more peaceful but otherwise unknown land. Maybe my parents shed a nostalgic tear but all I saw as we stood waiting to walk up what seemed to be an enormous and steep gangplank were lots of people milling about, dressed in their Sunday best – moustachioed men in suits and ties, sturdy, olive-skinned women in dresses and hats – as if on their way to church.

Once on board the *UV* for what was just its second voyage to Australia, our little family was split up because men and women were segregated into different dormitories. If mum and dad ever thought that this was an eerie echo of what had happened as their fellow Jews arrived at the death camps, they never said. Mum and I shared an eight-berth cabin in the lower deck with a bunch of other ladies who, I remember, used to hang their underwear on lines across the bunks. The journey took about six weeks, stopping at various ports including Naples and Port Said in Egypt, before sailing single file through the Suez Canal to Aden and Colombo in Ceylon (now Sri Lanka) and then southeast across the Indian Ocean to Freemantle.

The passengers were allowed to explore the various exotic ports while the ship was refuelled and stocked with fresh food and water. All the noisy, gesticulating Italian emigrants, plus we three Hungarians, would eagerly decant from the *UV* and haggle with the local merchants for souvenirs. I also remember being amazed when we arrived at Colombo at the dozens of small boats with traders, their heads wrapped in cloth, offering trinkets, ornaments and leather goods, even carpets! They would hold up items and barter with passengers on deck. Once a price had been agreed, a basket would be sent up to the buyer who would place the agreed amount in the basket.

After my father died at the age of eighty-nine, I found a pair of leather sandals he'd bought in Colombo almost exactly fifty years before. The strange sights and sounds and smells in these ports were both suspicious and seductive. I still have a photograph of the three of us standing in a Colombo street-market next to a UV officer carrying a briefcase and looking tall, handsome and very tanned in his crisp white uniform. I remember feeling bewitched by this exotic place, and even now I get the same sense of excitement when I'm on a cruise about to visit some port I've never been to before.

One very exciting moment during the voyage came when we crossed the Equator. The *UV* crew staged the traditional line-crossing ceremony that commemorates a sea-goer's first crossing of the Equator. The origins of this ritual go back to ancient times when sailors were superstitious and made entreaties to Neptune, the god of the seas, to bring them home safely. Thus, 'Neptune's Journey' has been a feature of immigrant voyages for centuries.

I had never seen anything like it before, and we watched in delight as the crew (and some of the passengers) dressed up in strange costumes and face-paint and created a sort of marine pantomime involving King Neptune and his court. The sailors invited passengers to take part and many boisterous Italian passengers volunteered. The pageant helped lift everyone's spirits and refresh us for the second half of the journey. Many modern cruise lines continue the tradition as a means of providing an entertaining spectacle for their clients.

But even in 1949, children were well catered for on board with endless games and fun events on offer – I remember making a valiant effort to win an egg and spoon race but dropped the egg almost immediately! It was very embarrassing, and I was terribly upset. But two teenage boys who slept in dad's cabin and who used to carry me around on their shoulders, came over and made a fuss of me, so I made a quick recovery!

As it was an Italian ship sailing from an Italian port, it wasn't surprising that most passengers were Italian, as were the crew, or that the food on board mostly catered for them. I was introduced to spaghetti for the first time in the *UV*'s large dining room. Initially, however, the food wasn't so good and, dad being dad, he organised a protest to the captain; as a result, we got more fresh produce, and milk was provided the kids. Wine was provided at every meal, including breakfast!

In fact, many of Australia's current Italian community can be sourced to those trips made by the *Ugolino Vivaldi* and its sister ships. Many had been given free passage provided they worked for five years. These hopeful emigrants fleeing the continuing chaos as the whole of Europe fought to get back on its feet, would lay the groundwork for what would become a quintessential, wonderful contribution to Australia's incredible multicultural heritage.

For example, a young girl from Lovero in northern Italy who boarded the *UV* in February 1950, would go on to become one of our country's most influential clothes designers and businesswoman. Carla Zampatti was just nine years old when she, her mother Marianna and two brothers sailed to Freemantle to join her father Domenico who had travelled to the goldfields in Western Australia a few years previously. And, at the time of writing, Carla's daughter Allegra had just won the seat of Wentworth in the 2022 General Election, standing as a so-called 'teal' independent candidate. Talk about the Lucky Country!

There are a few other things I remember about that long voyage: the first is the huge map that the crew put up on a wall in the main salon; every day they would move a pin on the chart to show where we were and how far we still had to go. Then there was the stormy day I was walking along the deck with my father when the tail of a cyclone hit, and the bow of the ship went under some huge waves; these crashed onto the decks, and we held on to the railings for dear life and laughed as we got drenched by sea water. It was like being in the front row at a Sea World show!

When we experienced what they call 'heavy seas', I remember feeling not so much scared as extremely excited. It was no wonder that the captain organised regular safety drills: "The ship's going to sink,' he'd shout through the ship's speakers, 'put your lifejackets on!" The first time he did that, I was petrified that we were going to drown, but after that, of course, I knew it wasn't for real.

And then, before we knew it, we were sailing through Sydney Heads and then on towards the Harbour Bridge; it was a lovely, sunny day – 30 May 1949 – and we were refreshed and ready for our new life.

Despite all odds, we had survived all that Hitler and Stalin had thrown at us!

CHAPTER 20

G'day Australia!

A SHOCK awaited us when we arrived at the dockside in Sydney: Dad's relative, the woman who had paid for our passage, had tragically died while we were at sea. Suddenly, appallingly, we had no Australian sponsor, no one to help us settle into our strange new country, and nowhere to stay after we had been processed. More to the point, we had just nine Australian pounds to kick-start our new life.

On the ship's manifest, our Australian contact was listed as 'C.G. Moore, Flat 11, 210 Victoria Street, King's Cross'. Presumably, that was the address of dad's cousin, but we could no longer stay there. At that moment, my parents must have thought they'd jumped from the frying pan into the fire. After the traumas of the previous few years, we were now homeless and almost penniless on the other side of the world – sixteen thousand kilometres (and light years away in other respects) from the familiarity of Europe.

Undaunted and ever pragmatic, dad promptly contacted the local Jewish Board and they found us a room in the back of another family's home. I've no idea who these kind people were or where their house was (other than it was near the airport) and I have no real memories of our short stay there. I do, however, still have a photo of me and my parents smiling in front of a picket fence in the garden; in it, they already look Australian – my father is wearing a short-sleeved shirt, shorts and sandals, and my mother a white frock and two-tone penny loafers; I am smiling in a sundress and clutching a rather ugly doll which sports a mass of tight blonde curls.

A few years later, we would further demonstrate our commitment to Australia and our new life by changing our surname by Deed Poll. Thus, my father had three different names during his lifetime: he went from Kohn to Kalmar to ... Kent. From then on, I was known to friends and family as Suzi Kent, which I thought was very chic!

To make ends meet as our new life Down Under began, dad got a job packing boxes, while my mother went to work sewing in a clothing factory. A priority was learning the new lingo and they went to night school to learn English. I was also sent to have lessons and dad's first question to my tutor was typically direct – "How do I stop the child from having the Hungarian accent, you know!" The same man told my parents never to use English with me at home, so I would not end up speaking it with a Hungarian accent.

Years later, long after I'd left home, I would call them every day, and we would still speak Hungarian. The strange thing is – Hungarians almost never lose their accent – think Zsa Zsa Gabor. I had a cousin who was only about twenty months old when she arrived in Australia, never spoke Hungarian but learnt English from her parents and had a beautiful Hungarian accent. And hand on heart, that's something I would love to have today as a reminder of my roots.

Post-war Sydney was chalk and cheese with either Budapest or Vienna. The climate, the food, the architecture, the cars and people – all very different to what we had been used to. I'd love to say that the Aussies made us immediately welcome after all we'd been through, but sadly that wasn't the case. We were 'bloody reffos' and that was all there was to it. That said, it was lovely to see much fewer soldiers and police around and, perhaps as a consequence, the city's atmosphere was so much lighter and less intimidating than we had been used to of late. And, of course, there were no burnt-out buildings or debris in the streets.

Both my parents thought the food in those days – mainly based on the British 'meat and two veg' approach to cuisine – was awful. They said the bread was like cardboard, and the milky tea was undrinkable; they didn't know what to do with porridge – so they put salt on it and ate it cold. Both really missed not having good coffee (remember, this was more than fifty years before Australia became obsessed with the stuff, so my father was ahead of his time!). Dad was particularly grumpy about this outrageous situation and was only satisfied many years later when a fellow Hungarian opened a coffee shop in King's Cross where he roasted his own beans.

My mother, who had been used to having maids cook for us, had arrived in Australia with few culinary skills, but somehow got hold of a Hungarian cookbook, and, with the help of friends, she soon became quite proficient. I still remember her specialties: duck or chicken livers cooked in chicken fat (which I could not stomach today!), and my absolute favourite – chestnut puree. In winter when chestnuts were in season, she would buy two kilos and we would spend all of one Saturday rubbing our fingers raw as we peeled them before tucking into the delicious puree topped with lashings of whipped cream.

At least the meat and produce were in reasonable supply. Wartime food rationing in Australia had mostly ended by the time we arrived, although butter and tea were still being rationed until 1950 (note: the UK still had rationing until 1954). In those days, there were more pubs than restaurants or cafes. It would take a few more years before the full, fabulous impact that the mass emigration of Greeks and Italians would have on the dietary habits of Australians would kick in.

However, Greek cafes and milk bars were already springing up everywhere. The older versions did not serve Greek food, instead catering to Australian tastes: meat pies and hot chips, steak and eggs; mixed grill and with lettuce, tomato and beetroot, tinned spaghetti on toast, sliced white bread and butter, and tea.

The newer establishments had a more American feel, with names like 'Monterey' and 'The Atlanta', and offering hamburgers, ice cream sundaes and milkshakes. As one commentator said at the time: "The Greek café was a Trojan horse for the Americanisation of Australian eating habits. With their round art-deco windows, and often next door to the picture theatre they were a marriage between food and fantasy."

This was certainly a world away from the rich, heavy Hungarian food we had been used to with its emphasis on poppy and paprika, and items like *kefir* (a fermented milk drink) and *quark* (curd cheese), thick soups and stews, and a host of potato-based side dishes.

Television was yet to arrive (1956 in time for the Melbourne Olympics), there were few house phones; most women didn't work. They stayed home to cook meals, and to clean, sew and iron. Few Australians drank wine on those days. Blokes drank (a lot of) beer, women had shandies or sherry; shops closed at 5:30 pm on weekdays and at 12:30 pm on Saturdays. Nothing was open on Sundays including petrol stations, pubs and grocery stores. There wasn't even any sport. Apparently, you were meant to go to church, come home for a roast dinner (at lunchtime), wash the (Holden) car, do the garden, then go out for a Sunday drive and perhaps a picnic.

The year we arrived, 1949, posted a record for immigration. The influx of different nationalities brought an unprecedented multiculturalism. The word 'cosmopolitan' was used, possibly for the first time, to describe Sydney and Melbourne by Aussie journalist, Sarah Dunne in 1950:

> "Little Australian children are learning and playing side by side with school fellows from many lands. Foreign voices, foreign languages are heard daily on the trams. Continental cakes and foreign foods are in sale in every city. Australia is growing up and becoming more cosmopolitan."

Alas, however, that still did not stop we emigrants being called 'wops', 'dagos' and 'reffos'!

In the middle of the twentieth century, Sydney was already a large city – Australia's biggest – with a population of 1.6m in 1950 (compared to 5m+ today). Refugees and immigrants like us helped swell that figure for the next few years as the city opened its doors to tens of thousands of 'ten-pound poms' and other people like us from southern Europe, all eager to start a new life in the land of opportunity; every week a liner would steam into port with more hopefuls, and the wharves of Woolloomooloo, Sydney Cove, Walsh Bay and Pyrmont would once again ring to a medley of strange accents.

I still appreciate the majesty of the architecture in continental capitals like Vienna, Prague and Budapest, but to me as a seven-year-old, Sydney's light-filled spaces and amazing seascapes, and its more relaxed wood and glass structures seemed so exciting and exotic compared to the stuffy, suffocating classical architecture and gothic, soot-stained buildings I'd been used to in Central Europe. As one brochure from the time put it: "Australia offers the attractions of space and opportunity,' while another one said that 'Sydney has an ever-present holiday atmosphere." 1950 also ushered in a new era of optimism and economic prosperity as the newly elected Robert Menzies government negotiated new trade deals with the United States and Japan.

At some point, we moved from our rented room to our own place in the eastern suburbs of Sydney; Kingsford was, and still is, I imagine, a down-to-earth but pleasant residential slice of suburbia within easy reach of the city's many attractions. It is close to beaches at Clovelly and Maroubra and surrounded by parks and several golf clubs as well as the Royal Randwick racecourse.

Today, the main cultural and culinary influences are Asian, with many of its residents being students at the nearby University of NSW, but Kingsford still has St Spyridon's, a Greek Orthodox church, as a nod to the suburb's past.

We lived at 82 Edgar Street, a quiet tree-lined road abutting Latham Park which is now part of Maroubra. It was a small, two-bed, semi-detached bungalow with rendered walls and a red-tiled roof which we first rented before buying it sometime later. There was a gas burner to heat the water, and the washing was done in a copper tub with the help of a wooden stirring stick and a hand ringer. It's strange what one remembers! I also recall being given my first dog, a beloved wire-haired fox terrier who I called 'Mucki'.

Then, in 1959, we had an unexpected bit of luck: my mum won six thousand pounds in the Opera House lottery. This was a huge sum in those days and more than the prize money that Danish architect Jorn Utzon, received when he won the international competition to design the iconic landmark. This miraculous windfall enabled us to move to a posher house in Douglas Parade, a short street in Dover Heights between Bondi and Vaucluse, and close to the water. From the clifftop, you could see both the city and the Harbour Bridge. Interestingly, according to the 2016 census, Dover Heights has the highest percentage of Jewish people in Australia. I suspect the same was true when we lived there sixty years before.

The sixth of April 1955 was a proud day: we became Australian citizens. Dad is described as a 'merchant' on his certificate while mum's occupation is listed as 'house duties' on hers. I don't think the latter would be acceptable nowadays! As a sidenote, the official signature on the document belongs to Howard Holt who was then the Minister of State for Immigration. But he would become famous a decade later when he was Prime Minister and disappeared while swimming at a beach in Victoria, sparking various conspiracy theories.

In the meantime, I too was drowning ... not in the ocean but at school.

CHAPTER 21

Lessons in life

BECAUSE OF the war and its brutal aftermath, my formal schooling had been a bit lax by that point. This became a priority for my parents. By now, both were working long hours at their new jobs in Sydney, and I was left on my own a great deal, there being no one else to look after me.

As usual, my father came up with a solution. He had told a Catholic man at the box factory that we had converted to Catholicism during the war, his colleague suggested that dad approach the church authorities about my education.

After checking the confirmation papers issued by the church of Krisztina Varos to my parents in 1943, they agreed to send me to a Catholic boarding school at no cost until my dad became established. A miracle indeed. The fact that neither of my parents were religious didn't matter, but the proviso was that I would become a Catholic. "I didn't care about that," my father told me decades later, "I just wanted you to get a good education."

The upshot was that I was sent to St Mary's Convent in Maitland, a town in the Lower Hunter Valley just north of Newcastle. I have a vivid memory of travelling there on a steam train, my mum and I sitting on wooden benches that were filthy from the soot coming through the window. The school was more than one hundred and fifty kilometres away and it was a long, tiring journey. We were both very nervous and, when we arrived at the convent, we clung to each other for mutual comfort in the waiting room.

For my part, I was terrified at being separated again from my parents, and I guess she was remembering the last time I'd been sent away – I ended up dirty and lice-infested in a stranger's barn! My mother was white-faced and close to tears, and I remember saying to her rather bravely: "Don't show them that we're afraid."

By "them" I meant the Dominican nuns; they looked very forbidding as they bustled about in their flowing white habits and scapulars, their black veils lined with white cloth, and the distinctive tall coifs that covered their heads being squared off on top. But I quickly learned that, though earnest and occasionally stern, most were good women and fine teachers. One even used to give me a box of groceries to take home with me for the holidays.

But, overall, St Mary's was not a happy time for me. I still shudder when I think back to my first day: I was taken into the refectory and introduced to everyone as the school's first 'refugee'. My body shook as I stared down at the sea of faces.

It didn't help that my English was still rudimentary, and this led to a good deal of bullying and name-calling by the other girls. Throughout my time at St Mary's, I never really felt accepted, and it didn't help that I had many stints in the infirmary wearing mittens due to mosquito bites that became infected.

The only happy memory I have from those days is of St Dominic's Day which is celebrated on the fourth of August every year: we had sports events and concerts, and special treats, including being allowed to watch a movie up in our dormitory with all the beds pushed together. The nuns would relax the normally rigid rules and I recall being astonished to see some of the girls, normally so well-behaved, roller-skate down the polished concrete cloisters and climb the mulberry tree in the picturesque gardens.

One other bit of excitement from my first year at Maitland comes to mind: the Hunter Valley was severely flooded and six people in the region were drowned. The water came right up to the first-floor dormitory, and we were all evacuated; I have a clear memory of being taken on a small boat to stay temporarily with a family in Cessnock. When I rang my parents to breathlessly tell them about this remarkable event, my father joked that this was becoming something of a habit, as I'd been evacuated once before from the orphanage in Miskolc!

Music was a big thing at St Mary's but despite the fact I enjoyed music I was tone deaf and was asked NOT to join in choir practice as I put the other girls off! I cringe when I think back to the end-of-year concerts – I was included in the choir but told to just mouth the words! So, during choir practice, I'd go to the library instead, and this gave me a lifelong enthusiasm for reading. When I was a bit older, at another boarding school, it would get me in trouble because I started reading books that the Catholic hierarchy did not approve of; this led me to question some of the church's dogma and resulted the school writing to my parents and urging them to stop me reading this seditious literature!

Looking back, it's a blessing that I have only suffered occasional nightmares and jarring flashbacks to our travails in Hungary and Austria. My resilience probably came from the fact that at that time I was concentrating on the here and now, just trying to get by, rather than dwelling on the tortured past. Nevertheless, I was miserable at school; it felt like I had been abandoned in a foreign country, among foreign people. I never really managed to fit in, and I missed my mum and dad terribly, along with my precious pup Mucki.

It was a great relief when, after a couple of years at Maitland, I was sent to another Dominican boarding school that was much closer to home – Santa Sabina College at Strathfield. That meant I could be a weekly boarder and see my parents most weekends. But even then, I wasn't really that happy; there was no privacy in the dormitories, the beds were placed head to toe, and we had to line up to use the washing facilities. I was always hungry, and

I sometimes sneaked out and pulled vegetables from the side gardens to nibble on. When I returned from visits home, I used to hide food in my bag to eat in the following days.

On the other hand, it is only fair to say that the dedicated nuns at both these schools provided me with a very good all-round education, with many valuable life lessons – even if their religious fervour could be very daunting to a little Jewish girl! But I did come to like the hymns and the theatre of the Mass. I had my confirmation the first year I was at St Mary's and the assumption was that I had already been baptized in the Catholic faith. To this day I don't know if I ever was – it never came up in conversation with my parents and I never asked.

But I do remember worrying a great deal as I lay in my dormitory at night that my parents would go to hell because they were not proper, practising Catholics!

CHAPTER 22

Revolution and a family tragedy

DESPITE OUR eagerness to embrace our new homeland, dad continually kept a close eye on what was happening back in Hungary. Not surprisingly, he had no love for the Soviets who had forced him to leave his home and business to escape torture and possible death at their hands.

He believed their imposition of the Stalinist system on the country of his birth, now called the Hungarian People's Republic, was an abomination and hoped that one day it would be dismantled. It would take another thirty plus years for this to happen, and a great deal more dirty politics, death and drama would have to play out first.

In our absence, the communists, now led by Matyas Rakosi, an avowed Stalinist, had taken up where the Nazis had left off with regard to oppression, persecution and thuggish tactics. In 1949, his socialist government tried and convicted the Catholic Cardinal Jozsef Mindszenty for treason, claiming that he had collaborated with the Germans in their Holocaust campaign.

Soon after, Rakosi's AVH security police, 'relocated' twenty-thousand Hungarians who were so-called 'Western agents' and allocated their homes to communist party members. The detainees were either sent to concentration camps or deported to Russia. Many, of course, were never heard of again.

The communists also targeted the Hungarian intelligentsia, nationalists and bourgeois elements who opposed the imposition of what amounted to socialist brainwashing in schools and universities; this resulted in widespread unrest and discontent throughout the country.

No doubt dad read of the death of Joseph Stalin in 1953 with some glee. What he could not have expected, however, was that it would have a domino effect that would ripple through the Soviet Bloc and result in a spontaneous uprising – the Hungarian Revolution of 1956. It started innocently enough as student demonstrators marched through central Budapest to the Parliament building. They were fired upon by the AVH from within the building. The news spread quickly, and disorder and violence erupted throughout the capital.

Once again, the already battered Budapest was subjected to the sight of Red Army tanks on its streets as the Russians moved to brutally crush the Magyar revolt. Thousands of protesters and political activists were arrested and twenty-two thousand were sentenced and imprisoned; another thirteen thousand were interned and estimates suggest that more than three hundred Hungarian were executed. Approximately two-hundred thousand refugees fled the country in the aftermath, many of them following our earlier example and heading to safety in Austria.

Among them was my father's older brother, Ferenc (whom we called 'Ferri') and his family – wife Gyorgyi, and son Robbie. The latter, who was then just ten years old, once told me that he remembers walking home one day with some friends when they heard gunfire all around them; they ran into a building and hid under a table. After it was all over, he went out in the street and stood next to a Russian tank, before being told to "get lost" by a Russian soldier.

Ferri's decision to leave Hungary was also driven by two other factors: first, the cloud of 'palpable fear' created by the AVH that that all lived under, and second, what he described as the 'virulent anti-Semitism they were still experiencing more than decade after the Nazis had been driven out of his country. The final straw came when the whole Kalmar family was out walking one day, and they were verbally abused because they were Jewish.

So, in 1957, they decided to leave Hungary. Typically, the callous principal of Robbie's school found out about this and offered to help – but only if they gave him their nice apartment. Ferri and his family retraced our steps by taking a train to Vienna, where they spent a month in an apartment before boarding the SS *Toscana*, another Lloyd Triestino ship – in Trieste, and arrived in Australia on 30 May 1957. The Menzies government had initially offered sanctuary for up to three thousand Hungarian refugees, but this was subsequently raised and, before the end of 1957, a total of fourteen thousand 'fifty-sixers' as they were known, had arrived in Australia.

By this time, I was fourteen years old and a pupil at Sydney Girls High School in Moorpark, having just moved there from Crown Street Intermediate High School. Several decades before the rise of social media, news and world affairs then largely passed teenagers by, but the Hungarian Revolution was different – it was a big story worldwide, pitting East against West, and there was a lot of excited chatter about it in the corridors and classrooms, possibly because the revolt was started by students only a little older than themselves. So, for once, my Hungarian background gave me some degree of status among my peers.

I remember we were all so excited as we awaited their arrival on a similar ship to the *Ugolino Vivaldi* in May 1957. We hadn't seen these family members for nine years. But just as we had received a shock when we had landed in Sydney in 1949 to learn that our relative had died, we were confronted by yet another calamity – my uncle Ferri had suffered a serious stroke just as his ship was docking. My parents had to watch as he was stretchered off unconscious and put in an ambulance and taken to hospital. Tragically, he died the following day. He was just fifty-three.

Ferri had been a professional musician, playing the trombone in a band called 'The Bill Boys' that must have been at least modestly successful because it performed in many different countries. He had been married to Gyorgyi (nee Grunwald) for twenty-five years and they'd lived in Budapest for all of that time. They'd also owned a small store located near their apartment in Kossuth Lajos Street that specialised in elegant ladies' gloves.

According to my mum, my uncle looked nothing like dad. She said he resembled the French actor Charles Boyer with his dark piercing eyes and dark hair. With regards to Gyorgyi, mum described her as an elegant woman, also with dark colouring, who looked like a softer version of Wallis Simpson. Robbie, a handsome boy, inherited his parents' dark good looks.

Shocked at her husband's unexpected death, Gyorgyi and her son lived with us in Kingsford for about a month before moving into a small flat in Randwick. She then went to work, first in the Hestia bra factory and then as a receptionist in the medical practice of our family doctor Frank Darvas, a lovely man.

Like me, she married three times in all, her second husband, with whom she had started a 'schmatta', or rag-trade enterprise, dying of a heart attack on their doorstep. Gyorgyi lived to the age of ninety-five before passing away in 2004, having also outlived her third husband who was a dentist. I saw her from time to time over those years. She was an attractive, elegant woman but not an easy lady to get on with.

Robbie, meanwhile, went to Catholic boarding school in Sydney for a short time but he was miserable there just as I had been at St Mary's, and his mother took him out soon after. It could not have done him any harm, however, because he went on to become a doctor, married a New Zealand girl, Vicky, and they had two sons.

The Kalmars have lived in several country towns and now reside on the Gold Coast. Sadly, we have not been close cousins since our childhood, although we have met and been in contact at various times over the decades. More recently, I've reminisced with Robbie about the contents of this memoir and the family history it tries to portray. Like me, he wishes he had learnt more about the events that shattered the country of our birth and shaped our lives.

CHAPTER 23

My Jewish awakening

FOR MOST of my childhood, 'being Jewish' had never really figured in my consciousness. The subject was rarely mentioned at home, and I had been educated at Catholic schools. My parents seldom went to the synagogue or observed any of the rituals or traditions. We did not eat kosher food. And, despite excelling at Bible Studies during my stint at the Maitland convent, I'd never been very interested in either the religious or cultural aspects of my Hebrew DNA.

So, it came as a bit of a surprise to me (and my parents) when, around the age of fifteen I suddenly developed this itch to discover more about the Jewish faith and its roots. Looking back, I now think it was probably sparked by the fact that we were mixing socially with a lot of other Jewish families, many of them, like us, originally from Hungary.

These people were more prone to practise the festivals and rituals such as keeping kosher in the home, observing *Shabbat* (the sabbath) weekly and celebrating *Hanukkah* and *Rosh Hashanah* annually, while fasting on *Yom Kippur* and observing family rites of passage such as *Bar-Mitzvah* and *Shivah* (the seven-day period of mourning after the burial of a deceased person). We also went to a number of weddings and, as a young girl with burgeoning romantic notions, I was greatly intrigued by the Jewish marriage ritual and its rich Hebrew symbolism.

Although I was now feeling much more comfortable at school (one year I had even been selected to give the Anzac Day address), and with my new Australian identity, I told my parents that I wanted to learn more about Judaism; this included discovering more about the Torah, the Hebrew bible, and the ancient laws and principles rooted in *halakha* (the path that one walks) that were established around 500BC.

I was surprised that my father, after his initial shock, seemed rather pleased. The post-war immigration had brought large numbers of Holocaust survivors to Australia – proportionately, more survivors than any other country apart from Israel. Some, like my father, were not interested in religion of any kind, while others said with some bitterness, "Hitler killed my faith". But dad was a huge supporter of Israel, and I guess he thought my new interest would give me greater insight to what the massive progress that this new country was making at that time, and perhaps greater pride in my Jewish roots.

Soon after, he asked their good friends Andrew and Anne Sved, for advice. Their son George was preparing for his Bar Mitzvah – the ceremony that marks the time a boy becomes a Jewish adult – and they recommended that I should see the rabbi who was supervising his learning.

Dr. Alexander Grozinger was the rabbi at the relatively new Maroubra synagogue a short distance from our house, and I started seeing him on Wednesday afternoons after school. He was then in his early forties, a most gentle, delightful man. He was also a Hungarian and had been in Budapest during the Nazi occupation with his wife Magda where they helped the Zionist resistance to save other Jews.

One of Magda's relatives, a man called John Grunstein, later wrote that the young Alex had also worked with Raoul Wallenberg helping to provide protective false papers – known as 'Schutz-Passen' – for Jewish fugitives. Alex and Magda, who was only a few years older than my mother, left Hungary in 1948 and spent two years in France with the firm intention of moving on to Israel but fate intervened in the form of his ongoing health issues, and they ended up in Australia instead.

So, this man was no dry, dusty cleric whose only interests were sacred texts and religious doctrines. He (and his wife) had *lived* and had also risked death for the sake of others. In other words, a bona fide, three-dimensional hero. When my mother and I visited his home near the synagogue for my first lesson, I remember Dr. Grozinger smiling as he promised, in a thick Hungarian accent, that he would not try to overwhelm me with religion, but he hoped that I would learn to read Hebrew (not an easy language to pick up) and learn about such things as the Jewish High Holy Days and when you break the bread and light the candles.

Every week for about a year, we would sit in the rabbi's study which was an enclosed veranda at the back of the house. We sat opposite each other in armchairs in a relaxed manner; mine used to face bookshelves on the wall that also contained a large Menorah. He was very easy to talk to, and, when I think back to those times, I treasure not just the calm, compelling conversation but also the shared experience with my mother who also enjoyed learning about Jewish history and where we had come from.

It amuses me to remember the time that the rabbi urged me, in his soft voice, to strive to be a good Jewish wife who could say the prayers at the Friday night Shabbat. His teaching must have worked because I duly reconverted to Judaism and took the name Miriam. And, somehow, that gave me a boost in confidence as we increasingly socialised with other Jewish families and individuals. These included:

The Sveds, who I mentioned above, had had their own traumatic experiences during the Hungarian Holocaust. Andrew had spent a year in Auschwitz but finally escaped when he and a group of prisoners were marched into the forest; a Romanian guard whispered to him that the Germans were going to machine-gun them, and he should move to the back of the column. As a result, he was able to peel off and scramble into the woods.

Everyone loved Andrew because his glass was always half full: everything he did, everything he saw and everything he ate was "just the best". His view was that he had already been to hell and so now everything in life was wonderful. His wife Anne, who we called 'Anci', was my mother's best friend and they spoke every day either in person or on the phone. Their son George and I grew up together and we remain friends to this day. The two families used to spend Sunday nights together enjoying a great spread of salamis, European cheeses, home-made pickles and the only hot dish, baked potatoes; we also went on many joint holidays until my mother became ill.

Leslie Schwartz was my godfather, and he had the most amazing but harrowing tale to tell: "When I got off the cattle truck at Auschwitz and standing in line to go to the gas chamber," he'd say to a rapt audience, "Josef Mengele was making his selections. I recognised him as we had studied medicine together in Munich. He also recognised me and pulled me out of the line. I was put to work in the hospital." But that was all Les would say about it; he never spoke of what he had seen at the death camp or talked about Mengele who was known as the 'Angel of Death' due to his sick experiments on prisoners, including young sets of twins.

After Auschwitz was liberated, Leslie lived in Szekesfehervar, a small city near Lake Balaton about sixty kilometres southwest of Budapest. He was a dentist and we used to visit him for the day whenever we needed our teeth fixed. One day he told me, "You would be a pretty girl except for your nose. I'll pay to have it done when you reach seventeen." Not surprisingly, that had made me self-conscious about my looks! Well, Leslie was a lovely man and he continued to be my dentist in Australia but when I became seventeen in September 1959, he had clearly forgotten his promise and my parents had to fork out to have my nose reduced during the school holidays.

Tommy Tycho was a cousin of my father who had also emigrated to Australia, along with his wife Eva, who became an Australian icon. The son of a well-known Hungarian soprano, he had been a child prodigy on the piano but, arriving in Sydney in 1951, he was forced to find work in a factory. My father was worried he might damage his hands and lent him money to buy a piano and, through a friend, found him a job playing in a Hungarian restaurant.

Tommy's talent was such that he went on to forge an extraordinarily brilliant career in the entertainment industry in his adopted land on both stage and television as a musician, conductor and composer. He worked with all the top Australian artists including Peter Allen, Olivia Newton-John, James Morrison and John Farnham. The maestro also played with visiting stars such as Frank Sinatra, Louis Armstrong and Shirley Bassey and wrote scores for films including *Young Einstein*.

In the decades that followed, he conducted all the ABC symphony orchestras and was awarded both the AM (Member of the Order of Australia) and the MBE (member of the British Empire), but perhaps his most lasting legacy is the backing arrangement he made of *Advance Australia Fair* which, to this day, routinely used to accompany singers at major community and sporting events.

Over the years, we would see Tommy and Eva, an opera singer, occasionally; one time he gave us tickets to visit the set of the Mavis Bramston comedy show which was popular in the sixties, to watch him perform. After he retired in 2008 after a stroke, dad would visit Tommy regularly at his apartment in Bellevue Hill where they would chat away in Hungarian.

Footnote: Rabbi Grozinger died in 1966 at the relatively young age of fifty. He had suffered ill-health for much of his life. His wife

Magda lived until she was 103 before dying in 2021 – just as I embarked on this memoir. An extraordinary woman, she was more than merely a rabbi's wife – she was a senior pharmacist, a mother and grandmother who, like her husband, was beloved of the Kingsford-Maroubra Hebrew congregation.

CHAPTER 24

London calling, and marriage mismatch No 1

RABBI GROZINGER finally got his wish – seven years later, I became a good Jewish wife (well, sort of) and learned to do all the stuff that good Jewish wives need to do in the home, including reciting prayers on a *Shabbat*. However, he would have been less impressed if he had lived to see his protégé get married a further twice – and to Gentiles, at that.

I might not be in the same league as other Hungarian ladies such as Zsa Zsa Gabor (nine marriages), or even one of her sisters – Magda (six) and Eva (five), but I can picture the gentle rabbi stroking his beard and saying sorrowfully, "... no, no, my dear, that is not 'megfelolo' (proper)."

I was in London with my friend Lillian Upton when the fateful phone call came from my father setting off a chain of events that would lead to my first marriage. This is how it all happened ...

After Sydney Girls High, I had gone to the Metropolitan Business College in Margaret Street, Sydney to do secretarial studies (as one did in those days). Lillian, who was also Hungarian, became a fast friend. We were both hopeless romantics and captivated by the breath-of-fresh-air social and cultural changes that the Sixties had ushered in.

We hatched a plan to travel to England together once we got jobs and had saved up enough money. I already had a healthy bank balance having worked in my school holidays – variously in a cake shop, a dress shop and then in the little tobacconist kiosk at Circular Quay that my parents owned.

In early 1963, Lillian and I boarded the SS *Fairsky* in Sydney, and embarked on our great adventure. The *Fairsky* has a unique place in the history of Australian immigration, having brought many thousands from Europe, including ten-pound poms such as former Prime Minister Julia Gillard and her family. Her Labour colleague, Anthony Albanese, now Australia's PM, also has good reason to remember the *Fairsky*: his father Carlo was an Italian steward on board the steamship and met the politician's mother in 1962 on one of the cruises.

Over the years, many future Australian stars making their way to the northern hemisphere to seek international fame and fortune, would play their music on the *Fairsky* including The Seekers and the three Gibb brothers who would later become the Bee Gees.

Lillian had wanted to go via Singapore as an English school friend, Peter, had joined the British Navy and was stationed there. They managed to meet up and, much later on, after I'd returned to Australia, they got married in England. Peter eventually became the chief engineer on the nuclear submarine *Warspite* before retiring with the rank of Commander and going to work at Whitehall. Nowadays, she and Peter are still very active and spend a lot of time cruising around the Greek islands in their boat.

I had left home with a large trunk and two suitcases, as Mum had made sure I took lots of my beautiful, tailor-made clothes. Sadly, however, by the time the ship docked in Southampton, after a six-week trip, I had put on so much weight I couldn't fit into my extensive wardrobe!

This came down to two things: the plethora of pasta on the menu, and the heap of chocolates that Lillian had brought. Her father was a director of the company that made the immensely popular Red Tulip chocolates and he had given her a couple of two-pound boxes to take to England; only one of them made it! Arriving in London, I had to park my redundant clothes in the basement of a small hotel in Bayswater that belonged to a friend of my father's; I was only reunited with them when I headed back to Australia several months later.

We had waved goodbye to Sydney's warm spring and arrived in London to find the UK experiencing its coldest winter in two hundred years; we didn't mind the temperature because London was fast becoming the hottest place on the planet during what would be become known as the Swinging Sixties.

It was the year that ... The Beatles released their first Number One hit *From Me to You*, followed by *She Loves You* and *I want to Hold Your Hand*. It was also the year that more than twenty-one million people watched their refreshingly irreverent performance on the Royal Variety Show that year – the one when John Lennon famously said "... those in the cheap seats should clap their hands; the rest should just rattle their jewellery!"

Also, in 1963 ... Christine Keeler and the 'Profumo Affair' changed the face of politics, *Doctor Who* began screening on television, and *Glamour* magazine named Jean 'The Shrimp' Shrimpton, as their model of the year. Meanwhile, Mary Quant was busily changing the face of world fashion and the audacious Great Train Robbery also captured the headlines.

One of the highlights of my UK sojourn was the wonderful job I landed with a large architect/interior design company called Dennis Lennon & Partners in Manchester Square, near Selfridges. Lennon was well known for decorating sets for the Glyndebourne opera, designing the interior of the QE2 and many other high-end architectural projects. He once employed design guru Terence Conran after he left the Central School of Arts & Crafts and several years before he opened the first iconic Habitat shop in Chelsea in 1964 and changed the face of interior design forever.

A remarkable highlight came in May, when the company was given the job of decorating the foyer at the Royal Opera House in

Covent Garden for a royal visit by the King and Queen of Belgium, and I was part of the team that spent a couple of days putting flowers into a wall in the lobby.

For my hard work, I was given two tickets (in the gods) to attend the event, and Lillian and I stood breathlessly as the guests, including Queen Elizabeth, her sister Princess Margaret, and the Duke of Edinburgh, arrived in beautiful evening clothes and adorned with glittering tiaras, medals and jewels. It was, to say the least, a memorable evening for two rather dowdy young Australians.

The pair of us lived on a shoestring but we still managed to save enough to go to concerts or take weekend trips to different parts of the country. We spent Easter in Scotland that year; despite it being April, it was still snowing there. We stayed in a dingy, draughty Edinburgh youth hostel and afterwards I said to myself – never again!

Things brightened up considerably when my parents' friends, the Sveds – Andrew and Anci – came to London that summer. I took a week off work, and we went out every night to dinner, the theatre or a concert. This was a great change from the relative austerity that I had been used to since arriving in London.

The Sveds were great fun and, inadvertently, caused a bit of a scandal at their hotel. One night it was very late by the time we had been out and had a late supper. "It's too late to go back to your place," they said. "You must stay with us." Well, in the morning one of the hotel workers came to the room with a breakfast trolley. His eyes popped out of his head when he saw Andrew in bed with me, and then Anci appearing from the bathroom! As a result, Andrew became a celebrity with the male staff in the hotel, which tickled him pink.

All too soon it was time for the Sveds to leave London and I settled back into my normal routine as a girl about town, working hard and partying when I could. In my head, I figured that I'd be there for the foreseeable future, if not forever. But then, just before my twenty-first birthday in September, the phone call from my father changed everything.

It was shattering news: my beloved mother had suffered a heart attack!

The journey home was frantic and frustrating. Dad had wired me the cash to fly back. But the aircraft broke down twice – first in India and then in Darwin where the passengers had to be put up in Nissan huts for twenty-four hours. I only had a small bag with me and was dressed in a knitted dress; I remember lying on the bed in my underwear in the terrible heat, worried out of my mind that my mother might be seriously ill ... or worse.

On arrival at Kingsford-Smith airport, I went straight to the hospital. To my surprise (and relief), my mother was in relatively good shape – which is more than could be said for me: I was nearly eighty kilos and had a tooth missing; my mum nearly had another heart attack when she saw me! Her hand flew to her mouth, and she burst into tears. Guess what I was given for my twenty-first present? A year's subscription to a health studio! Subtle, not.

Being back at the house in Dover Heights was bittersweet. It was lovely to be with my family again, especially my mother. But, during my absence, several friends had got married and I felt left out. It didn't help that my father continued to treat me like a child and made several sly digs at my single status. At least my visits to the health club paid off because I slimmed down to my normal weight in just a few months.

Once I'd got my figure back, I started socialising in earnest. Among the people I hung out with was a confident young man called Ivan Ungar who was a couple of years older. He was over six foot, slim with black-framed glasses; in our wedding photos, he looks like Hank Marvin from pop group The Shadows, only more handsome. To begin with, we were just mates, but during the long weekend in July 1964, when he and I were sitting around playing cards, Ivan casually came out with a bombshell proposition: "We're both from the same background," he said, "you've travelled, and we make a good pair. Why don't we get married?"

Well, talk about knock me down with a feather! This had come out of the blue, and at first, I thought he was joking. But he was serious. Did I love him? Not really. I doubt he ever loved me either. But he was attractive and, to be honest, I was desperate to leave home – after the freedom I'd enjoyed in London, my father was driving me mad. Many of our friends were either already married, or were engaged, and so it seemed the natural thing to do. Bottom line: I accepted Ivan's proposal.

His parents, with whom I got on well, were delighted. As were mine. We all started planning the wedding and where we would live. But it wasn't all roses: I still remember our family GP, Frank Darvas, coming over on the morning of our engagement and warning me that Ivan would not make a good husband. But I stupidly ignored him and carried on with our plans.

My friend Lillian came home that Christmas for a visit, and I thought it would be lovely if she could be my bridesmaid, so we set the wedding for early February 1965. We got married at the Temple Emanuel in Woollahra, which nowadays has the largest Jewish congregation in Australia. The reception was at my parents' place, the usual wonderful Jewish spread organised by our two mothers along with Anci Sved. Mum played the piano and there was singing and much joy.

I look at the wedding photographs now and marvel at how happy we all look. Ivan, tall and smooth in his smart tuxedo, sports a huge smile. But, in fairness, I too am smiling in my white tailored dress with a small train. And thank God, I appear very slim – the dreaded Red Tulip chocolates a distant memory by then!

Sadly, the smiles would soon fade.

CHAPTER 25

Innocence

OUR MARRIAGE started off well enough. We bought a small, two-bedroom apartment in Kingsford and furnished it with a mix of new and second-hand furniture, the latter donated by our two families.

Ivan was a very good salesman with a charming personality and a smooth line in chit-chat; at the time we got married, he worked for a company that made leather wallets and other small leather goods, but soon after I suggested starting our own similar venture. My father lent us two thousand pounds (dollars only arrived in Australia in 1966) and we set up a company called 'Baron and Baroness' in Rushcutters Bay along with another partner who was a leather craftsman. The enterprise took off quickly, but I had to work three jobs so that we could pay dad back.

We hung out with a great group of friends, particularly a couple called Claire and Phillip Marco (whom I still know to this day). We'd all go to the movies and spend many Saturday nights playing Canasta until two in the morning or go dancing at the Hunters Lodge in Double Bay.

It seemed to me that we were having a ball, but my innocence and lack of experience with men meant I was oblivious. Unfortunately, it did not take long before Dr Darvas's dire warning was borne out. When I confronted him about our relationship, he just shrugged and said, 'Look, it's you I love'.

After a year or two of this, I told my father I wanted to divorce Ivan, but he urged me to try to make a go of things. The upshot was that we remained married for four years. At one point, because of the anxiety and low self-esteem that I was suffering as a result, my mother even asked Ivan's parents, Rosie and Imre Ungar, to talk to him.

The Ungars had also been in Budapest during the occupation and its aftermath, and had experienced similar trauma: like my father, Imre had been pressganged into a slave labour battalion while Rosie and the young Ivan went into hiding. They and their sons had come to Australia after the Hungarian uprising in 1956.

All in all, it was a dark, miserable time for me, perhaps not as tortuous as my childhood experiences in war-ravaged Hungary, but the toxic marriage had quite a debilitating effect, sapping my confidence and pushing me towards depression.

Ironically, I loved Ivan's family including his younger brother Thomas who is now a renowned concert pianist and music professor in Texas. Tommy, a lovely man, always said that I married the wrong brother!

My in-laws were practising Jews, but not overly religious. That said, Ivan and I nearly always had *Shabbat* dinners at their home on a Friday, with the usual rituals of the lighting of the candles, Hebrew prayers and the breaking of the *halah* (bread). They always celebrated *Pesach*, or Passover, and would get us seats in the synagogue at Bondi for *Rosh Hashanah* and *Yom Kippur*. My mother-in-law would tell me to go and buy a smart outfit with hat to wear to the services. She also taught me how to cook different Jewish dishes, a skill I regrettably no longer have.

By the middle of 1966, I had saved up enough money to leave Ivan and live on my own. And that was my intention. But yet again my father persuaded me to make one last bid to keep our marriage together and, against my better judgement, we used my 'escape fund' to pay for a sort of second honeymoon in Europe, the prelude to a fresh start.

After a short stint in London visiting friends like Lillian and Peter, we travelled on to Budapest. There, we were shown around by my mother's delightful old friend Dini Molnar, who by now was married to a doctor. We checked out my family's old apartment in Deak Ferenc Street (where we had hidden in the crawl space) and visited some of Ivan's relatives.

It was a largely depressing experience; the heavy hand of the communist regime had reduced this once majestic city to something of a slum with unkempt buildings and dirty streets. The grey brutalism of the Soviet architecture and the bullet-scarred walls near St Stephen's Basilica also contributed to the city's air downtrodden air. The taxis smelt of boiled cabbage, stale body odour and cheap cigarettes. The Hungarians we met only had enough hot water to bathe once a week, and had limited access to good food and drink, other than vodka.

In contrast, when I returned to Budapest a second time in 2002 with John, it was rather shocking to find that this postage-sized patch of inner city on my tourist map was now the bright, beating heart of a modern metropolis with a myriad of high-quality attractions; a vast, varied mass of people – locals and foreigners – browsing the upmarket stores; families picnicking in the parks and everyone seeming happy and prosperous.

It was staggering to think that a city so steeped in blood, so shrivelled by Nazi and Hungarian fascist atrocities, and so smashed by Russian bombing could rise again from the ashes, almost as if nothing had happened, as if hundreds of thousands of innocent Hungarian citizens had not been treated as subhuman and sent to their deaths. I remember thinking that the scale of evil perpetrated during this dark chapter in the country's history should have left some indelible stain on the city, its buildings, and its people, obvious to all visitors. But I saw no sign of it.

That earlier trip with Ivan was designed to help save our marriage, but it failed. In the cab on the way home from the airport, the hit song on the radio was Nancy Sinatra's *These Boots Are Made For Walkin'*. Very apt because soon after, I made a final and irrevocable decision to leave the marriage.

Our friends, some of whom I still know to this day, were shocked; outwardly we had been the perfect couple ... attractive, outgoing and building a successful business together. People in those days kept their feelings and emotions to themselves, their secrets tightly wrapped; social media did not exist – no Instagram or Twitter to tempt us to tell the world our innermost thoughts and feelings. Our friends and acquaintances therefore had always assumed Ivan and I had a rock-solid relationship. How wrong could they be!

The truth was that I had come to feel somewhat inadequate – my parents had survived so much heartache and upheaval in their lives, yet still shared an unshakable bond. Why couldn't I have found the same with Ivan?

Confession time: in the final year of our marriage, I am not proud to say that I started a love affair. In my defence, I was a wreck by this time and in desperate need of emotional support. He was a much older, sophisticated man called Oscar, whose own marriage was also unstable. Our affair was more spiritual than physical; we used to meet for coffee before work almost every day and he would write me the most beautiful poetry.

After my divorce, Oscar declared that it would be unfair to marry me as he was so much older. At the time, I was upset but he was probably right; we remained close friends until he died, and I'll always be grateful to him for single-handedly restoring my self-confidence and giving me a shoulder to cry on.

Footnote: Like me, my first husband went on to marry twice more. The first was to a girl with a law degree he met in Hungary and brought to Australia; they had a daughter before divorcing. Ivan then married a lovely Australian lady, and at the time of writing, they were living in Coogee. My own real contact with him in the time since was when I called him to offer my condolences when his parents died.

CHAPTER 26

Mismatch No 2 and a heartbreaking tragedy

INEVITABLY, OUR divorce was a scrappy, long-drawn-out affair with Ivan proving very difficult. No surprise there. In those days, it was not as easy as it is now. Basically, one person had to be cast as the guilty party.

After much drama and stress, I went to my parents' house, collapsed on the sofa, and couldn't walk for days. Ivan continued to resist and, with the stress of the whole long-drawn out, daggy drama, I did a stupid thing – I signed over all our assets to him. This left me with very little money. Fortunately, my soon-to-be ex-husband's parents, Rosie and Imre, were aggrieved by my situation and, God bless them, once again gave me a helping hand.

With their help, I rented an apartment in Bondi. My poor mother was again unwell at this time, so dad was busy caring for her, plus he had business problems of his own that distracted him. Meanwhile, I had a rather dull secretarial job in the city, most of my married friends were getting on with their lives, and I felt very alone and unloved for many, many months. I was only twenty-seven, but I began to feel my life was over.

And then one day, while visiting some friends, I was introduced to a man called Bill Weigall. Initially, I was not attracted to him – I was still licking my wounds after the failure of my marriage – but he was very persistent. Bill would pick me up from work, go shopping with me, and when I came down with the flu, he insisted on staying at my place to nurse me.

Things went from bad to worse when my father took a shine to him; I should have known then it was doomed to failure! To be fair, Bill was very well-educated, a real gentleman from an illustrious old Australian family; his great uncle Albert Bythesea Weigall was Sydney Grammar School's headmaster for forty-five years – its sports complex still bears his name. His family also included prominent lawyers and barristers.

Bill was tall and fair-haired and looked Scandinavian, although I think his family originally came from England. Quite early on in our relationship, he said he wanted to marry me. I was hesitant; having already been stung once with Ivan, I was in no hurry to try again. Besides, I knew I was not really in love with him. But Bill's mother was dying of cancer, and he kept on at me, saying that her dearest wish was to be at our wedding.

Once again, my father weighed in. He had been won over by Bill's charm and urged me to take the opportunity to marry into such a good family. So, I finally gave in, and we got married on the seventh of September 1971, less than a week before my twenty-ninth birthday.

To be fair, Bill was charming and caring, and a great communicator. Unfortunately, he was also a bit of a dreamer, with grand ideas but without the ability to follow them through. As one of his friends told me, "Bill builds castles in the sky and then moves into them."

In the early days of our marriage, he had a succession of jobs with mining companies before starting subdivisions in the country that were successful for a while. His mother died and we moved into her old apartment in Bellevue Hill and started up a fledgling real estate business in Lane Cove with another partner. We were coasting along comfortably enough but then I became pregnant.

This was a wonderful surprise. I had suffered from painful endometriosis since I was thirteen-years-old. This can impact fertility. Through a friend at Sydney University, I was referred to a sympathetic gynaecologist, Dr Andrew Child, who said that I needed an operation if I ever wanted children. And, lo and behold, after major surgery, I conceived very quickly.

Bill was delighted and, against my wishes, he immediately decided to buy a beautiful apartment in Darling Point which I didn't think we could afford. But we moved in and happily prepared for the arrival of our child. And then tragedy struck – at six months, as the baby got heavier, my cervix started to open. The hospital put me on a drip to try to stop the premature delivery.

The next thirty-six hours were harrowing, made worse because we could hear the baby's heartbeat which seemed to be normal. As my contractions progressed, Dr Child was called in at around four in the morning. Soon after, my baby was born. The staff tried and failed to save him, and I lost my son.

This was, naturally, devastating for both of us, and compounded by the fact that, in those days, neo-natal babies who died were simply taken away and 'disposed of' by the hospital. I was not allowed any time to be with him or hold him, and to my everlasting regret, I don't have any photographs of my child. We still had to register his birth and we named him Tony. To this day, I do not know where my little son was buried or even where he was taken by hospital staff. It was all a terrible blur. All I do know is that this precious little person was given an autopsy because I was given a certificate to that effect although we were not given any details resulting from it. The document, which I still possess, is dated the tenth of March 1975.

Nearly fifty years later, I still get choked up thinking about it and how callous the whole process was in those days. The doctors and nurses presumably thought they knew best, and the less that bereaved parents knew, the better. It was as if the birth had never happened, that I had not carried my son with love and joyous anticipation for one-hundred and eighty days. Instead, the silence and awkwardness that hung over my hospital room seemed to suggest that something shameful had occurred, and it was best forgotten.

I am damn sure that none of this would be allowed to happen in the modern era, that grieving mothers and fathers are treated with more respect, and allowed to spend time with their babies, mourn them properly and have them buried or cremated with due ceremony.

Back at Darling Point, I fell into a deep depression. The usual stuff: I could not get up in the mornings, just stayed in bed crying for about a month. In the meantime, Bill lost money on a mining venture, and we had to sell our beautiful apartment and move to a smaller one close to Bondi Junction. When I was physically able, I got a job as secretary to the managing director of a real estate company in the city. Then the pattern repeated itself: Bill got involved in another 'pie in the sky venture' and again I got sick from all the stress and the lingering mental anguish from the death of my baby.

It was probably the worst time of my life, even worse than when I was at my wits end with Ivan. Finally, I decided that my health would continue to deteriorate if I stayed with Bill. I rented a room in an older lady's apartment for $10.00 a week and put my furniture into a friend's garage.

Bill went off to Asia with his tail between his legs. I still have a most beautiful letter he sent me, saying how sorry he was that he had made a mess of our life, how he still loved me and planned to return when he had made enough money. Bill would later have two more children with an Australian woman before marrying a much younger Indonesian girl. He died a few years ago while fishing in New Guinea without ever having realised his dream of making a fortune.

Now, if close my eyes and think back to the time I was alone in that rather sparse lodging room, I can remember suddenly feeling free, and a person in my own right. The fog of depression that had hovered over me for months began to lift and I became much more positive about my future. It was my strong and certain belief that, after two horrible, failed marriages, I would one day find my true soulmate.

And, you know what? I did. More of that soon. But first, I had to make a living.

CHAPTER 27

Suzanne of The Strand

NOW THAT I was on my own again, and almost penniless, I needed to support myself. Up until then, I'd only had one job I'd really enjoyed; it was immediately after leaving secretarial college. I'd gone for an interview at Revlon cosmetics in Rushcutters Bay and landed a position working alongside make-up artists and the PR people.

The head of the department was a very colourful fun guy who dressed in flamboyant clothes. Now, of course, I realise he was probably gay but at that time I was still naïve, and that sort of thing wasn't talked about. Things have certainly changed since – and a great thing too.

It was a good time. I learned how to apply make-up which has stood me in good stead ever since. Well-known artistes, like Lanie Kazan, an actress who later appeared in *My Big Fat Greek Wedding*, and Australian singer Lana Cantrell, would drop by the office and give us tickets to their shows. Every month we could buy cosmetics that were seconds in the factory at heavily discounted prices, so I was a good supplier to many of my girlfriends. I loved that job and was sorry when I quit to go overseas with Lillian.

When I returned from London to see my mother, I embarked on a succession of dull temp jobs, working for senior managers of different companies – mostly large ones such as Bristol Myers Squibb, an American pharmaceutical company which in those days had offices in Goldfields House at Circular Quay. I also worked for the National Secretary of the Australian Hotels Association.

After my marriage to Bill was over, I landed a short-term dream position that lifted my spirits. The famous impresario, Michael Edgley hired me to be his assistant when he brought the Bolshoi Ballet to tour Australia in 1976. The star of the company was Maya Plisetskaya, the Bolshoi's *prima ballerina assoluta* who was Jewish. In a career that lasted more than fifty years, she danced with such luminaries as Rudolf Nureyev and Mikhail Baryshnikov.

My job was to take notes at both the rehearsals and performances for Michael; that meant being stationed in the wings and behind the scenes at regular intervals. It was breathtaking and I had to pinch myself regularly. The demanding work also meant that, pardon the pun, I had to be on my toes every night.

I'll never forget Plisetskaya's tour de force triumph in her signature *The Dying Swan* at Sydney Opera House in August that year. Work on the landmark building still had not been completed and the famous sails had not yet been erected on the roof, so the makeshift stage was open to the sky. The stunning performance was televised and beamed around the world. It was a huge blow when the Bolshoi tour ended – Plisetskaya went back to Moscow, and I went back to more 'meat and potatoes' office work.

But, irrespective of a job being dull or exciting, I always believed in working very hard and giving total loyalty to my bosses; one of my strengths was my networking skills (perhaps because of my Jewish DNA!), and I'd make good contacts in different departments and then be able to keep my boss informed about what was going on, and who was doing what to whom! Most of the managers or directors I worked for during those years became family friends and, although it sounds sexist now, their wives would involve me in buying theatre tickets and presents, including neckties, for their spouses.

Later, I worked as the private secretary to Robert Salisbury, the MD of an old-established real estate company in Martin Place called Hardie & Gorman. Again, it was a hugely enjoyable, diverse job and I relished being part of a prestigious firm slap-bang in the middle of the CBD; apart from my normal secretarial duties, I organised lunches and hosted large functions. From memory, there were about forty employees and a great team spirit, thanks in no small part to the Friday night drinks parties. This camaraderie provided me with a much-needed anchor after the split with my second husband. By then I had also drifted away from the Jewish orbit that had circumscribed my life before Bill.

Over the first few years with H&G, I developed a great working relationship with Bob Salisbury and his wife Barbara. However, I gradually began to feel that my talents were being wasted as a secretary. At the time, the company was growing and diversifying and, when it ventured into shopping centre management, I thought that it was time to put my hand up for a promotion.

The new business included the beautifully rebuilt Strand Arcade between Pitt Street and George Street, and the row of shops on Margaret Street leading into Wynard. It had a new manager, and he needed an assistant. I talked to Bob about applying; he wasn't too keen on me moving on and, besides, the director in charge of the new department thought I would not be able to cope with the demands of the job.

His chauvinist comment is still etched on my brain forty years later: "If an attractive tenant asked Suzi out, she might let him off paying the rent." Scandalous – if that happened now, I'd be able to sue the company and have the man fired. However, I persevered, and when the new manager, Jeff Seddon, started, I kept nagging him to be his assistant, especially as, by then, I understood how the politics of the company worked.

Finally, he caved in, and I moved to the shopping centre department, having no idea what to expect but very excited to get out from behind a desk. Jeff took me under his wing, and it didn't take me long for me to become a good negotiator, to the point where tenants often came to me for help. I do think women have a better understanding of people's problems, but let me be clear – I never, ever let anyone get away without paying their rent!

In fact, there was remember a jeweller called Robert Clerc, a Swiss-born tenant on the first floor of the Arcade who was struggling with his rent. At a meeting, the decision was taken to have him evicted. But I suggested I talk to him first and see what could be worked out. The jeweller then started paying back rent in small amounts, and then formed a partnership with a very smart lady; they became so successful that he took a double shop on the ground floor of the Strand Arcade before moving into the Queen Victoria building.

Robert would go on to open a gallery and showroom for his stunning jewellery and sculpture collections in a building in Woollahra that he bought. Along the way, he won many design awards, and was commissioned to create the Tall Ships trophy. We remained good friends and, when my third (and final!) husband and I became engaged he made my engagement ring. Imagine what might have happened to him if I'd stood by while he was thrown out of the Strand Arcade because of a minor cashflow problem?

In the absence of a personal life, the heritage-listed Arcade became my passion. It had been built in 1894 but had become dilapidated, but after a fire it was restored to its former Victorian-style splendour in 1976. A newspaper feature in May 1980 described me as the "Centre manager with the feminine touch". It outlined my responsibilities as "... being secretary for the Merchants Association for both the Strand and the CBA retail section, rent collection, new rental negotiation, and oversight of the cleaning and security of the building. She also has to approve shop layout plans for new tenancies". The newspaper also mentioned that I was busy taking courses in business communication, business management and advertising at Sydney Technical College.

Then, my working life took an interesting turn. The producers of the Bernard King show called us out of the blue. Bernard was an actor, celebrity chef and TV personality who became a judge on the daytime talent show *Pot of Gold*, and later on *New Faces*. He was a pioneer of television advertorials in Australia, demonstrating the use of sponsors' products. And that's how I became a (sort of) TV star.

We were asked if someone from the company would come on his show and talk about the newly opened Strand. Jeff Seddon suggested that I should do it. I wasn't so sure; I was a behind-the-scenes kind of person who was more interested in supporting my managers and colleagues than grabbing the limelight. But my boss egged me on and, soon after, Bernard's manager came to interview me to and check my suitability. She was also a redhead and we immediately clicked.

They allocated me ten minutes airtime, and I came up with the idea of taking pieces of merchandise from the different shops and explaining about the uniqueness of the tenants. I was very nervous as Bernard was both witty and acerbic. In the event, he was very kind to me, and we really hit it off, even lunching together after I got married again.

It was a big hit for the Strand in 1979 as almost every shop that I featured had customers saying they had seen them mentioned on Bernard's show. When the Merchants' Association was formed, the tenants decided they would like to sponsor ten TV segments during the year; as a result, I became the presenter of a program called *Suzanne of the Strand* for three years. It was great fun but took a lot of organising especially as I had to feature every shop during the course of a year.

The high-profile TV appearances helped boost both my confidence and my status in the office, and a young woman, Phyllis O'Brien who was thirteen years younger than me, was then hired to take over my secretarial duties. She was also going through a separation, and I helped her settle in. The pair of us had great times together, going to the gym in our lunch breaks, sharing beauty secrets and going out on joint dates. We became lifelong friends and to this day Phyllis remains one of my closest confidantes.

She came to see me in Noosa just before my eightieth birthday and, before she left, gave me a lovely letter that made me cry; this is how she remembered our time together at Hardie Gorman:

> "You were very much respected (and admired from afar) by the men in our office. The women just wanted to be you, but sadly we were not as genetically blessed. You were kind and supportive of me and found the time and patience to mentor me. I even recall once going to the swimming pool at the Hilton Hotel in George Street Sydney. With your long slender body and mane of titian hair, my beautiful Hungarian Jewish friend shone bright and always turned heads. Yet you remained oblivious of the impact you made. You taught me 'how to do life' and gave me a depth of friendship I couldn't imagine being without. I cherish the bond we have together. You are one of a kind! I love you, Suzi."

I love you too, Phyllis. Your friendship has been a constant and continuing light in my life.

On the surface, that was one of the happiest periods of my life – I was in my thirties, single and not unattractive; my social life had never been better; my confidence and self-esteem were high; and the stress and strain of two failed marriages was mostly behind me. But underneath, it still felt as if something was missing.

Then one fateful day, I remember it so well, the twentieth of June 1982, my boss organised a 4pm forum on shopping centre maintenance for the BOMA (builders, owners and managers association), with four guest speakers. I was reluctant to go as I was not involved in the boring maintenance side of the business. Thank God I changed my mind and walked in after the meeting had started … otherwise, my perfectly pleasant but rather ramshackle existence would not have changed in the incredible way that it soon did.

CHAPTER 28

The air-con guy and the redhead

THERE IS a well-known inspirational quote, attributed to Buddha, I believe, that says, "Failure is a part of life – if you don't fail you don't learn. If you don't learn you'll never change."

Well, I'd had my share of failures when I met a special man at that shopping centre maintenance seminar in June 1982, and I guess I must have learned from those screw-ups because he and I have now been married for nearly forty years.

A less romantic event to meet one's soulmate is hard to imagine but, hey, that's karma or serendipity or fate or probably just sheer bloody luck! The man was at the BOMA 'Four o'clock Forum' to speak about air conditioning, a subject I knew nothing about, and cared even less. My first impression of this stranger was not helped by the fact that my boss, Jeff Seddon, had pointed to him earlier and joked: "Look at that guy in the middle of the room perving on your legs."

I looked up and there was this man with a plate in one hand, fork in the other, almost missing his mouth with it as he stared at me. Maybe it was the short black skirt, black stockings and skyscraper heels that I was wearing. He later told me that, for him, it was lust at first sight! Later, we were introduced by one of the BOMA officials and we chatted for a while but when I left to go home, I did so without a further thought about the man who would soon transform my life.

I was about to celebrate my fortieth birthday, and was still, to some extent, licking my wounds. I was still wary of relationships with men after my two failed marriages and careful not to get too attached to someone just for the sake of having a partner. In my heart, what I was looking for was a man who was intelligent, caring, had similar values to me, and secure in himself – someone who was established and enjoyed life. Working in the city, and a being woman in mainly a man's world, I had plenty of dates, many of them successful men. However, I had a self-imposed rule that if after the second lunch there was no 'spark', I prefer to go out with my girlfriends.

So, when the 'air-con man' rang me a few days later, I didn't know even who he was. He said his name was John Smeed and mentioned that he'd met me at the BOMA session, and could he take me for lunch? I demurred, saying that I already had plans. Fifteen minutes later, the phone rang again, and Mr. Smeed said he'd moved some appointments around and could he meet me later for a drink? Wow, I thought, he's keen! So, I rang Jeff Seddon, told him about the call, and asked, "Which one was he?"

He laughed so loud, I had to hold the phone away from my ear. 'He's the one who was looking at your legs!" Jeff finally replied. That verbal exchange remains a family joke, and we tell people about it to this day, just as I am telling you the reader. Well, to cut a long story short, John and I had lunch soon after. I'd love to say that Cupid shot an arrow straight into my heart and I heard angels on their golden harps, but frankly, there was no real electricity, at least on my part. Indeed, when I returned to the office, I described him to my secretary as "a rather boring engineer who is into meditation". The meditation thing had come about a couple of months earlier when John had quit a three-pack-a-day cigarette habit and suffered dramatic withdrawal effects and behavioural changes. Just as well he'd done so, because there is no way that I would have gone out with a smoker. Our relationship would have turned to ashes immediately!

Nevertheless, a week later John asked me out again, this time to the Manor House in Balmain; I remember sitting in the side room with an enclosed veranda with the sun streaming in. The conversation flowed, and suddenly there was the lovely man I now know and love with all my heart. He was articulate and interesting, and showed me great respect.

When I mentioned that I hated the cold and was hoping to go on holiday somewhere warmer, he asked me where I was going; off the top of my head, I said Vanuatu and he immediately said, "Let's go together." I laughed, of course ... but what John did not realise was that he'd just passed my two-lunch rule, and we continued to go out together at the expense of my girlfriends.

As the weeks went by, I became more and more attracted to him. One day, when I had to go to Wollongong to do a TV show, John said he would take me in his Porsche. Later in the dark studio, he came up behind and gave me a hug. My senses just went 'bing'! On the way back, he asked me if my passport was up to date. Two days later, a ticket to Vanuatu arrived on my desk.

When we met, John was a few years older than me, and, although I did not know it, was similarly looking for some stability in his life after a decade of what he has described as a "wild 1970's bachelorhood".

On the plane to Vanuatu in August 1982, I still remember John deep in a discussion about fishing with the passenger next to him, and me thinking – this is nuts, I'm going away for a week with a man I haven't even yet slept with, and he's talking fish! My fears were short-lived, however – we had an incredible time together and, on the fourth night, while at a restaurant called 'Le Sur le Toi' (I still have a coaster from there), John was talking about Beethoven, and I suddenly thought ... this is the man I want to spend the rest of my life with.

My friend Phyllis approved. This is how she remembered those days of courtship:

"Then along came John! A truly beautiful man who fell quickly under Suzi's spell. They were in love, and I was thrilled for them. They both had their separate histories and baggage to contend with at the time, but their bond was solid, and they emerged stronger as a result. The incredible thing is that while their relationship was still taking shape, Suzi, kind and supportive of me as ever, took me along on her dates. Poor John didn't realise we came as a package deal!"

Returning to Sydney, my fellow workers used to laugh at me as I waited for his phone calls like a lovesick teenager. Then, at the end of September, I went to a four-day BOMA conference in Surfers Paradise with some colleagues, and on the final night John walked in as we were having dinner to surprise me. The conference organiser asked him what he was doing, and John declared, "I've come for the redhead!" That's John in a nutshell: strong, single-minded and sharp as a tack.

It was comforting to me that he had none of the negative qualities of my first two husbands. He didn't chase other women, and he was a doer, not a dreamer. I really liked the fact that he had already enjoyed great success in his field. After leaving Brisbane Grammar School, John had become a cadet in Queensland's largest general engineering company, Evans Deakin, which built large ships and locomotives.

For five years he studied four nights a week at what is now Queensland University of Technology, graduating in 1958 as a mechanical engineer. He had then moved around the multiple Evans Deakin sites to gain practical experience and an understanding, at grassroot level, of how the organisation worked.

This exposed John to the tough, hard-drinking and occasionally violent atmosphere found in shipyards and boiler shops. That 'character development' proved invaluable in the years ahead while he dealt with union reps and bullying building contractors.

"I learned how to swear properly, drink like a man and deal with physical threats," is how he put it.

In 1961, he had joined another company, York Air Conditioning, a subsidiary of a US corporation, first as a design engineer and then as Queensland Manager with a staff that, over time, grew to two hundred. He went on to spend time on projects in America, including a period working on the design of the huge refrigeration plant for the World Trade Centre in New York,

Then, in 1972, John decided to form his own successful air conditioning company, Siganto and Stacey, alongside another York executive Pieter Oosterhoff, and two others. Later, John renamed the company Optimus Pty Ltd and acted as chairman before selling it to Hastie Australia Pty Ltd in 2001; he continued as a Consulting Engineer with clients that included the Sydney Opera House and Atlantis, The Palm Resort in Dubai. In 1996, he won the Sir William Hudson Award, the most prestigious prize in the Australian engineering industry.

I mention all this rather boring business background to highlight three things: John is a successful entrepreneur, tough as old boots and twice as smart. As a former design engineer, he has always mapped out what he wants, and then goes after it.

And, thankfully, he went after me! Now, when I think back to our early courtship, it reminds me of the old movie *A Touch of Class*, starring Glenda Jackson and George Segal, about a couple who go away to get to know each other and, before they know it, fall in love.

We've now been together for four decades. I should mention that I wasn't the only one with a marital past: John had wed once before and had three daughters, but he had been separated for ten years by the time we met. At first, my relationship with his daughters Jane, Donna and Louise was slightly awkward, understandably so because they were very close to their lovely mother Pat, but soon I was made to feel part of John's extended family which now also includes beautiful grandchildren and great grandchildren.

I asked John early on why he hadn't had a divorce. He told me bluntly it was because he'd had no intention of marrying again. Well, I wasn't having that, and on our way back from a wonderful trip to South Africa where he had business interests, I finally decided, as an old-fashioned girl, that, if a man loves you, he should give you his name. If not ... well, I would have to consider my position. I don't remember ever spelling that out to John, but he must have somehow got the message because, at the end of January 1983, he went to Brisbane where his first wife lived and asked her for a divorce.

And then, on Easter Sunday that year, he got down on his knees (while we were in bed!) and proposed. And this was his proposition: he had tickets to Wimbledon in a few months' time, and we should get married in London while there. That was an amazing plan, and I was totally beguiled but I failed to do my homework because, when we arrived at Chelsea Registry Office, we were told that one or other of us had to have been resident in the borough for fifteen nights, or we couldn't be married. What an anti-climax!

Shocked and bitterly disappointed, we headed to Hawaii where we had planned to have our honeymoon. There we discovered that it was much easier to obtain a marriage licence, and in Maui we were wed in a Nissan hut on 3 August 1983 by a Hawaiian judge, with two of his clerks acting as witnesses. *Mahalo, Maui!* The beautiful island became our regular holiday haunt for many years after that, spending Christmas there fourteen times.

Thereafter, our life has been blessed, first in Sydney's Lane Cove and then for the last ten years in beautiful, iconic Noosa. I didn't realise it back then, but John represented something I'd craved my whole life up to then. God knows what a shrink would say about it, but I know now that John gave me the security I'd never really had; being rounded up in Papa and dumped in an orphanage before fleeing Budapest in the middle of the night is not a recipe for stability. And then, in Australia, I continued to have an unsettled life: two boarding schools, two marriages, one to a philanderer, the other to a dreamer who kept us on a financial knife edge. Then, to crown everything, I lost my baby.

John became my rock, a solid bulwark against all the demons from my past. I admired his generous nature and his willingness to allow me to look after our finances. I also loved the fact that, like my father, John had a love of classical music. While in Sydney, we had season tickets to both the opera and symphony concerts, and, when overseas, we often visited opera houses; my favourite musical memories are seeing *Aida* at the Colosseum in Verona, and our private tour of the Vienna state opera house.

Come to think of it, John is like my father in other ways … in addition to music, he loves reading newspapers and arguing about politics, and he's also pig-headed! I also have had a life-long interest in politics; I remember working for the Double Bay Libs when I was just in my twenties, handing out leaflets and manning poll booths. To this day, John and I both remain equally passionate about a number of political issues, including climate change and national security.

Does all this make my darling husband sound like a saint? Well, let me tell you that he's not! He's always had a bit of a short fuse, and for a while he drank a lot, albeit, being John, only fine wine. And, he can be infuriating in all sorts of other ways, not least because he was a workaholic who I had to drag out of his office on a Saturday afternoon to spend some time together.

Nevertheless, the 'air con guy' has been such a wonderful, caring life partner. Don't tell him this, but when I wake up beside him in the morning, I feel like pinching myself as he sits up and tells me he loves me while I gaze out over the beautiful sun-kissed water in Noosa. Oh my God, it is such a different planet to where I've come from – bombed-out Budapest, ghastly ghettoes and a desperate people facing genocide.

If the first forty years of my existence were turbulent and traumatic, the second forty have been a sea of tranquillity by comparison. John provided both the emotional and the financial security that I had never experienced before.

Yet life with him has never been boring; he has always been wonderfully energetic (still going to the gym in his mid-eighties), perpetually curious about people and places, and very sociable. We've travelled around the world, done some amazing things and made scores of fantastic friends since he 'came for the redhead'. Apart from a few health scares, common to people of our exalted age, we cannot complain.

Against the odds, my third (and final) husband has truly lived up to my beloved mother Erzsebet's deathbed prediction that he was "the one"; my one regret is that she was not able to see how my life finally became joyful. But I know deep in my soul that she would be so happy for me.

CHAPTER 29

Mum and Dad: life, love and loss

DURING THE seventies, while my career was in an upward trajectory there was one black cloud hovering above – my mother's health was in a downward spiral. This was immensely distressing to me. She had been more like my sister, my confidante, my best friend throughout my life, always wanting me to have things she missed out on when she was the same age.

She had her first heart attack in 1964 at the relatively young age of fifty, followed by a massive stroke ten years later, from which she never fully recovered. In the period between those two catastrophes, she also suffered from debilitating angina that slowed her down, and she underwent a full mastectomy. Throughout her health troubles, she never lost her positive spirit, except for the one time: it was after her stroke and mum was sitting at the dressing table; I watched her look in the mirror, and when she saw how illness had ravaged her, she started to cry. It broke my heart to see this once bright and beautiful woman reduced to a frail, unhappy shell.

Prior to this, my mother had been so vital and vivacious. And, as I sat with her, holding her thin hands, I thought back to the great parties we had enjoyed when mum would sit down at the piano and play Hungarian folk songs and Frank Lehar pieces; I still have a little cry when I hear *Vila* from *The Merry Widow*, one of her favourites.

Mum had a wonderful way with people. In my teens, when I'd

been at Bondi Beach with a bunch of friends, it was nearly always our home that everyone came back to, as Mum was so welcoming and always happy to feed a gang of hungry teenagers with homemade pancakes. After the 1956 Hungarian revolution, we shared our small two-bedroom semi at Kingswood with refugees, mainly young men, who arrived in Sydney. One of them became my first boyfriend. Even when I stopped going out with him, it was not unusual to come home to find him having coffee and a good chat with my mother.

In the Christmas holidays, like many Hungarians living in Sydney we went to the Blue Mountains; together with three other families we would rent an old boarding house in Blackheath. It was always a fun time: the wives would cook, and everyone spent time walking, playing cards, swimming; mum, George Sved and I used to go horse-riding together almost every morning. We would leave home at seven in the morning and walk the couple of miles to the stables, and then ride through the mist-covered bush. Great memories.

We also used to go to grand parties at the home of a friend of my parents who was a minor Hungarian aristocrat. His name was Kalman, but I don't remember his surname. He was not Jewish but had escaped Hungary around the same time we did; he, like my father, had offended the communists after some of their thugs had killed some Jews while intimidating voters during the last free elections held in Hungary during the Soviet era. The culprits were brought before a Magistrate who happened to be Kalman, and he was pressurised by the authorities to find them not guilty. Being an honourable man, he refused; soon after, someone in the Jewish community found out that he was to be arrested by the AVH, and he was smuggled out of Hungary.

Kalman had arrived in Australia with no money and because he could not practise law in this country, he went to work in the railways while he studied at night to become a librarian. He later worked in the Mitchell Library until his retirement. He was a tall, imposing man with a lovely deep voice; he spoke old Hungarian and loved to tell great stories. I remember him telling me that, before the war, he'd had a stable of horses on his estate and a pet wolf that ran beside him when he went riding. I think all the women had a crush on him. He was a great drinker and mum would sit at the piano in his house with a glass of wine and play Hungarian folk songs while we all sang along.

Mum was a very compassionate person and when someone in the community was sick, mum would always take a basket of food to their home and sit and hold their hand; her great warmth and empathy drew people to her. It was a terrible blow to her family and friends when, after suffering the stroke, forty percent of her brain was affected. She suddenly could not concentrate on watching the television far less read or knit or cook. Most days she could not even dress herself.

It was heartbreaking to witness her decline. Almost overnight, this caring, accomplished woman lost so much of her inner vitality and her innate beauty. Friends gradually stopped visiting because it was hard to have a conversation with her.

Fortunately, she still had rare moments when she was lucid, and I am so grateful that she was able to meet John before she died. We would occasionally go the apartment in Bondi Beach to have dinner with her and my father. But then, in late November 1982, mum fell and broke her hip; the doctors decided they couldn't operate as her condition was too weak and she remained in the hospital, in terrible pain. One day, she asked me if John would mind coming in to see her. I remember we went to the hospital one Sunday after John had learnt a couple of Hungarian phrases like, 'kezet csokolom' – 'I kiss your hand'.

Happily, she was lucid on that day and John was wonderfully patient and attentive as he chatted to her. When he left the hospital room, dad said that he wasn't happy about my latest relationship as he felt John was "too tough" for me. I was speechless, but my wonderful mother in stunning moment of clarity, as usual came to my defence – she said to him, "Look at Zsuzsiki's face! That is the man that will make her happy and the right man to spend her life with."

That is the last conversation I had with my mother, something that I keep in my heart. Soon after, she lost consciousness and on Tuesday, December 6, 1982, she died aged just sixty-eight. Neither of my parents were religious and mum was cremated, but in a nod to their Jewish heritage, dad asked Cantor Michael Deutsch from Temple Emanuel to officiate; he had a truly magnificent voice.

As I write these words, I almost weep as I look back on mum's rollercoaster life, with its sporadic highs and steady lows; I think of her courage, walking around Budapest without the yellow star on her breast; fleeing the Papa ghetto with me in her arms, and feeling devastated at having to leave her parents behind; living, first in the safe house, and then in the roof space in Deak Ferenc Street; searching for me in the ruins of the Hungarian countryside after the Siege of Budapest; and finally comforting me in the back of the mail truck as we crossed Russian checkpoints on our way to Vienna.

I also remember her determination to make their new life in Australia the best it could be, learning to cook and embroider – I still have a lace shawl and tablecloths that she made for me – and working long hours in the cigarette kiosk in Circular Quay, and putting up with my father's disappointments and dissatisfaction at his lack of business success. I treasure the memory of her great sense of humour, her warm spirit and her compassionate nature; for example, one day a frightened dog arrived at our door during a storm, and mum being mum took it in and cared for it. She took out an advert to find its owners who tuned out to be dog breeders, and they gave us one of their puppies as a sort of reward. This was Mucki who I mentioned earlier, and when my mother played the piano, the pup would sit beside her and howl, making us all cry with laughter.

After her death, I used to have lunch every Wednesday with Anci Sved, my mother's best friend, who I called my second mum. We often talked about her and one day, I asked her, 'Was mum really the wonderful caring person that I remember?'

And Anci, God bless her, smiled and said, "Even better than your memory."

While my mother's wonderful warm smile and generous, positive personality still haunt my thoughts forty years later, my memories of my father are more nuanced. From my childhood until his death in 1999, I was invariably at odds with him: he could be frustrating, overbearing and somehow could never accept that I was a grown-up woman.

He could also be brittle and argumentative. On the other hand, I still marvel at the devotion he showed to my mother during the long, distressing years of her ill-health. He had always adored her. And, from the time of her first heart attack when she was just fifty, dad cared for her wonderfully, from helping her shower and dress to organising the food and housework.

After her stroke, he hardly slept at night in case she got up for the bathroom and fell. I would often stay there at weekends just to allow him some respite. So, while it's fair to say he was not the easiest person, and we constantly rowed, he totally redeemed himself in my eyes by the way he made mother's last, difficult years as comfortable as humanly possible. They always spoke to each other in Hungarian and mum used to call him "draga elete" – "my darling life", while he, in turn, called her "szive" – my heart.

After dad died, I found a birthday card among his things that mum must have sent him after she got sick. It read (in Hungarian): "My darling life, I take this opportunity on your birthday to thank you for all the love and patience you are giving me. I ask fate to be as good to you as you are to me. I cannot wish for more. Millions of kisses, Erzsebet."

My parents were married for a smidgeon over forty-two years, and they shared a deep bond forged during the years spent being oppressed, first by the Nazis and then the Reds. The only time they had ever been separated was when dad was sent to the slave labour camp, and mum had to navigate the Nazi occupation on her own with a young child, knowing that he could be sent to the Russian front at any time. He, on the other hand, must have been frantic with worry that his wife and daughter had to fend for themselves. After they were reunited, they continued to love each other for the rest of their lives together, and I do not remember them even arguing that much, despite my father's prickly nature.

With the benefit of hindsight, I now reckon that his difficult character might have stemmed from his own challenging childhood. He had been very young when his father Isak Farkas Kalmar died from his wounds after fighting for Hungary in the First World War. His mother then died when dad was just sixteen leaving him an orphan; he and his older brother Ferenc had different personalities and did not get on well, so he was virtually left to look after himself.

He did so thanks to his self-reliance, determination and intelligence. He was not as outgoing as my mum, but he had an enquiring mind and educated himself, and loved to talk about politics and music. To his dying day, dad loved to read, was very passionate about current affairs, never missed the news, read the newspapers daily and had a great love of classical music – by the time he died he owned nearly one hundred and fifty classical records – despite Russian soldiers having stomped on his precious collection in our Budapest apartment in 1945! Dad also became an excellent bridge player.

He then built a successful textile business through hard work and commercial savvy before the war, and another one immediately after it. I believe his failure to replicate that success in Australia added greatly to his unhappy persona. He had arrived in his new country with just nine pounds but immediately started planning another business venture.

Dad's dreams of making a fortune very nearly succeeded but for two pieces of bad luck: first, he gained a management position in an Australian corporation, Reed Murray, that later offered him shares in the company when it diversified into property development. Seeing an unmissable opportunity to make his fortune, dad invested all that he had saved up by that time. The company subsequently went bust and dad lost everything.

His second bit of bad luck came in the early seventies when he then started a clothing manufacturing company with a female partner; dad looked after sales while the lady took charge of the factory and bookkeeping. Unfortunately, he found out too late that she was milking the funds and the company went into liquidation. Mum and dad had to sell the Dover Heights home to pay his creditors and it points to his character that he felt he could not let other people suffer for his misjudgement.

Despite the trials and tribulations of his life, my father soldiered on until he was almost ninety, possibly because of his rather cussed nature and the fact that he was still exercising twice a day! He had been a good sportsman all his life, rowing on the Danube while a young man, and playing golf in his later years. He only ever returned to Hungary once. It was some time after mum died, and he was extremely reluctant to go but John and I kept at him.

Dad kept inventing reasons why he couldn't go, finally telling me: 'I don't want to be spending your inheritance money.' Exasperated, I told him that if he didn't make the journey, I'd rip up $5,000 after he died and scatter the pieces in his coffin! That did it ... he went back to Budapest, and loved every minute of it, as I knew he would.

Still, it is a matter of some regret that my father and I somehow never enjoyed the close and affectionate relationship that I had with mum. Perhaps it was because the hard knocks he had experienced in his life had made his hopes and expectations of me overly high and I never quite measured up, while my mother was proud of whatever I did. I also regret that he was fonder of my first two rather feckless husbands than he was of John who, ironically, would give me the most wonderful life. Why was that? Well, I really believe it was because John was the first man in my life who was stronger than him and dad could not handle that very well.

Nevertheless, I would ring my father every morning to see how he was and when he lost his driving licence, I would take him shopping every week. When we lived in Sydney, John and I would take him to the Hungarian restaurant in Bondi for lunch every Saturday and occasionally to concerts at the Opera House. Fortunately (for both of us!), he was quite independent and kept himself busy, often visiting old customers from his days in the clothing industry. Even in his eighties he played golf twice a week and kept company with several Jewish widows.

On the morning of Monday, 15 February 1999, I rang dad first thing as usual. Getting no answer for over an hour, I rang a friend, a nurse who lived in the same building and asked her to look in on him. Soon after, she called back and said, "I'm so sorry, Suzi, but I found your father dead ... sitting in the lounge."

Just the day before, we had taken him to his favourite Hungarian restaurant in Bondi for lunch; when John and I got home there was a message on the answer phone from him, saying that he was listening to Verdi's *Requiem* and how much he was enjoying it. I think he would have appreciated the irony of his final choice of music.

So, it was of some comfort to me that he died peacefully and painlessly (of a heart attack) after a good Hungarian meal, while listening to his beloved classical records. He was eighty-nine.

It was a blessing that he never suffered like mum or, for that matter, had to go into a nursing home which he would have found intolerable. My father and I may have been at odds with each other for most of our lives, but I still loved him dearly ... and, God bless him, I know he loved me too.

To the end, dad treasured his cultural heritage. While not remotely religious, at his core, he remained a Jew through and through; his will reflected this, dictating bequests to various Jewish causes, including the Sir Moses Montefiore Jewish Home in Hunters Hill, the Australian Friends of the Hebrew University of Jerusalem, and the Jewish Centre on Ageing at Woollahra. It was an easy decision to have Cantor Deutsch sing at dad's funeral, just as he had done at my mother's.

Alav hashalom – peace be upon him.

CHAPTER 30

How I gained the courage to care

MY MARRIAGE to John, a Christian, caused one casualty – my involvement with the Jewish community. During the ensuing decades, my mother died, my father and I were constantly at loggerheads and my links to my old Jewish friends and cousins gradually subsided. It wasn't deliberate, I never consciously rejected my roots, it was just a consequence of the new life I had.

John was not responsible for this; in fact, he has always encouraged the Jewish part of me. He describes himself as a "Methodist Zionist" and is very pro-Israel. He also made a sizeable donation to the refurbishment of the Holocaust Museum in Sydney; we have our names on the honour board there.

But it was not until about 2012 that my interest in my Jewish blood was once again rekindled. I had been introduced to a lovely lady, Janet Merkur, the Co-Vice President of the National Council of Jewish Women of Australia (NCJWA) who, not surprisingly, had connections to both the museum in Sydney and its counterpart in Washington DC – the US Holocaust Memorial Museum. When she heard that I was a survivor, Janet asked me to do a video interview, telling the story that has been the subject of this book. Copies of that video were given to both those museums, and, a few years later, when we visited the one in America in March 2017, I handed over some family documents, which resulted in a thank-you letter from the museum authorities; while writing this book, they have also been very responsive to my research requests, as have *Yad Vashem*.

Shortly after that, I met a Hungarian lady who told me about an organisation called Courage to Care which visited schools and educated the students about the Holocaust. Its aims, she said, are to inform and educate Australians of the dangers of prejudice and discrimination. C2C was founded in 2011 by Andrew Havas OAM, a fellow Hungarian refugee. Here is why, in his own words:

> "One might ask what it means to be safe here in Australia; in Australia you live under the protection of the law not in fear of it. Where in more repressive regimes people live in fear, here the freedom of people is guaranteed under the law. People are generally not in fear of the 'knock' at the door in the small hours of the morning. Australia has given me the opportunity to be whatever I want to be regardless of financial situation or social status. I have opportunities to study, freedom of association, freedom to express my views and a bloody good way of life.
>
> "Most Australians share an immigrant heritage, living and embracing difference ... There is absolutely no place for divisiveness, discrimination or racism – attitudes which must be rejected. We are the world's most socially harmonious society, and we must remain that way. Thank you, Australia."

Stirring words, and when the lady told me that C2C teaches that ordinary people should not remain as bystanders to racist or bullying behaviour, it touched a nerve. I then made contact Kayla Szumer, the head of C2C in Queensland. Over lunch, she told me that there were very few survivors still living in the Sunshine State and therefore she would be keen for me to participate. Although in her eighties, Kayla is a lovely, lively lady who does a fantastic job of co-ordinating programmes and organising speakers to visit schools. She is helped by a great team of presenters, a few of them survivors, who are supported with banners, videos and props.

To be honest, I was hesitant at first – the thought of speaking to schoolchildren terrified me, and it also meant travelling to different parts of Queensland. But, after some thought, I decided it was imperative that the horrors of the Holocaust should be revealed to current and future generations, so I agreed to sign up.

First, two members of the C2C team were assigned to test my suitability; they asked me to do a presentation at my home. No pressure! Fortunately, I had put together a bunch of notes from my chats with my father before he died, and I also had some research material from my return visit to Hungary in 2002. They made some constructive comments about my presentation that improved its impact. More importantly, they told Kayla that I would be a valuable addition to the programme.

The first few times I stood up in from of the fourteen and fifteen-year-old students was daunting, but I quickly realised that my timidity did not matter – the vital thing was that the diabolical story of Hitler's 'Final Solution' had to be relayed to as many people as possible. And these kids had a very limited knowledge of the Holocaust

Now, as a seasoned veteran of such presentations, I take great satisfaction in being told, time after time, that the boys and girls have gone home from school and passed on to their families what they'd just heard. The result has been that often their siblings in the following years are eager to come to our presentations, and we know from the feedback from both students and teachers that C2C has taught them a great history lesson that they will never forget. Here's just one example of a teacher's response:

> "Suzi's survivor testimony was a gripping story of the trauma she lived which collapsed the time between the events of the Holocaust and the lives of the young women of All Hallows' School, Brisbane. Her story of survival and of her return to life after the Holocaust

here in Australia was a wonderful life lesson to a young audience. It is not only a story of a victim ... but a story about how to live as a victor. She made the phrase 'Never Again' a change-making call to action."

That teacher's name is Neal Quillinan, a lovely man, and I have kept in contact with him since that first meeting. He, and others like him, have helped make my involvement with the outstanding C2C organisation also change-making for me; in later life, it feels that I am doing something of real value for the community. I was also touched by the compassion many of the students displayed, often coming up me afterwards and giving me a hug. One girl called Ruth, a ninth grader, wrote to me:

> "Your story was moving, inspiring and encouraging. I learnt that a small act of kindness can change someone's life. Going forward, I know that I need to not judge others because I do not know what their past and present story is. And, I have learnt that I have the right to believe in my beliefs, my opinions and my goals."

John, fortunately, has been hugely supportive of my commitment to C2C, and gave me confidence as he listened patiently to endless practice sessions. I now revel in my personal Jewish history and am passionate about spreading the history of the Holocaust. There's another bonus: I get the opportunity to visit other organisations as well as schools, such as Probus, Rotary and book clubs, for example.

Along the way, I've met some incredible people – like Brigitte Gabriel, an inspirational Lebanese-American woman who grew up in war-torn southern Lebanon in the 1970s. Her Maronite Christian family was forced to live in a bomb shelter for seven years as the country was attacked by Muslim militants. She is now a conservative (and controversial) writer, journalist and political activist in the US who challenges and confronts fundamentalist Islamic teaching and jihadism. A *New York Times* best-selling author, Brigitte believes strongly that radical Islamism poses a major threat to Western values and culture.

Above all, despite being a Christian, she is a great supporter of Israel, and has addressed the United Nations on the subject of anti-Semitism. She has also been a regular visitor to the White House and has a million followers on social media. I've met her several times when John and I have visited the States and this pocket dynamo never ceases to inspire me with her energy and courage. She once told me that my work with Courage to Care showed that I was "fulfilling my mission in life" and that she was happy and proud that I was "changing hearts and minds".

Another inspirational figure that I met while working on this memoir, is Bert Klug, who is 100 years-old and, like me, a Holocaust survivor. Born in Slovakia, next to Hungary, he spent two years in a forced labour camp while his parents were deported to a concentration camp and murdered. He came to Australia in 1948 and trained as a doctor. We were both invited to attend a special announcement at the Queensland's parliament house on 27 October 2022. That was when State Premier Annastacia Palaszczuk revealed that her government was providing $3.5m towards the creation of a Holocaust Museum and Education Centre in Brisbane's CBD.

That sum was being matched by the federal government while Brisbane City Council was donating $500,000 to the project.

Likewise, I have been fortunate enough to become acquainted with Amir Maimon, the Israeli ambassador to Australia, a former IDF paratrooper and now a distinguished diplomat (more of him later). After we met at an 'Righteous among the Nations' event in Brisbane, he invited me to tell my story to a group of foreign diplomats and ANU students at the Israeli Embassy in Canberra on Holocaust Remembrance Day in 2022.

That event was an echo of the time that a director of Yad Vashem kindly invited me to attend a Holocaust memorial service in Israel. John and I felt privileged to accept. It was our second visit to this extraordinary country that has achieved so much in its seventy-five years of existence. The service took place on the slopes of the Mount of Remembrance in Jerusalem, and we were both reduced to tears when six holocaust survivors living in Israel told their story (on a screen) and introduced their children and grandchildren. Their poignant message was clear and concise: Hitler failed!

The next day we visited the curators at the museum to hand over pictures of my grandparents; they kindly showed me the original list of Jews in Papa that were rounded up and sent to Auschwitz with my name and that of my mother and her parents on it. I had previously been shown a copy of it by Mr Kiss on my visit to Hungary, but it still gave me the shivers to look at it.

Both my visits to Israel were almost spiritual experiences. On each occasion, for some time afterwards, I felt very affected by what I had seen and heard. It's hard to explain how I felt, but both the place and the people seemed to reach into my Jewish core and take me to a place where nothing could touch me.

My involvement with Kayla and the others was the result of that renewed pride in my Hebrew roots; that connection has truly given me the courage to care; and to fully and thankfully embrace my Jewish DNA. So much so, I was inspired to write this memoir as a lasting record of my microscopic part in a tragedy of massive and monstrous proportion; hopefully it might, in turn, inspire a few others to do the same. Here is one last comment from a recent attendee at one of my talks:

> "For me, and I suspect for many others, there were elements in Suzi's story which fitted within the distant menagerie of pasts. She could well have been speaking of my father's wife and their son, my grandparents etc who were in the same town, at the same time, likely to have been in the same dire straits. Clearly for me,

this was a personalised glimpse into my family's fate, yet the audience felt as much a part of her story, as if lived through Suzi's own experience. I am very grateful to have heard this story. Many more need to be told."

Yes, indeed they do!

The *Ugolino Vivaldi* and the passenger manifest list from 24 May 1949 listing our names.

St Mary's Convent in Maitland NSW where I boarded for a few years from the age of eight. It was not a happy time!

Above: The three of us looking like fair dinkum, true-blue Aussies after we became citizens in 1955.

Right: Mum, dad and I are safe at last, newly arrived in Australia 1949.

Shipshape: Me aged 20 relaxing on the top deck of the *Fairsky* on our way to Europe in 1963. The other photos show Lillian and I disembarking at Naples (left) and dressed for the 'Twenties Night' party on board the ship.

The changing face of Suzi: (above) at a glam ball in Sydney; (top right) a precocious pre-teen; (middle) shopping in Melbourne with the heroic 'Marta Haas' who had lived on the same street as us in Budapest while working for the Hungarian resistance; (bottom) my big hair and sunnies visiting London in 1966.

Top: The Gabor sisters, Zsa Zsa, Eva and Magda with their mother Jolie. Born of Jewish ancestry in Budapest before the war, they were the Kardashians of their day.

Above left: My father's cousin Tommy Tycho, musician extraordinaire.

Above right: Thomas Ungar, my first husband's brother, who became a world-renowned concert pianist.

Right: Maya Plitsetskaya the famous Russian ballerina, whom I met in Sydney.

Above: Ivan Ungar and I with my parents at our wedding in 1971. The smiles would soon fade.

Right: My second marriage to Bill Weigall also ended in divorce.

Below: Hat trick ... this was the first of three weddings. Ivan and I are surrounded by family and friends in formal attire. His brother Tommy, now a world-renowned pianist, is pictured back row, far right.

Top: With my mother and father, all glammed up for a social event.

Above: My parents with sister-in-law Gyorgyi Kalmar, whose husband Ferenc, my uncle, died after their ship docked in Sydney.

Middle right: Despite their different personalities, my mum and dad never stopped loving each other. She described him as 'my darling life'.

Right: Mum and her dearest friend Anne Sved whom she called 'Anci'.

Top: Overseeing the Strand Arcade in Sydney in 1980.

Above: On set with TV personality Bernard King as we spruiked some of my clients' products.

Left: My Strand colleague Phyllis, still a 'bestie' to this day.

Right: 'Suzanne of the Strand' glamming and hamming it up for the TV camera.

Above: John and I on our wedding day in Maui, 1983. Third time lucky!

Right: We have been lucky enough to share a thousand happy memories in our forty years together.

Top: Lunching at the Metropolitan Opera House in New York in 2022.

Above centre: John and I at Yad Vashem in Jerusalem, Holocaust Remembrance Day, 2019.

Above left: Visiting the Hungarian Jewish Memorial Museum in Safed, Israel, 2022.

Right: Touching the Wailing Wall in the old city of Jerusalem in 2019.

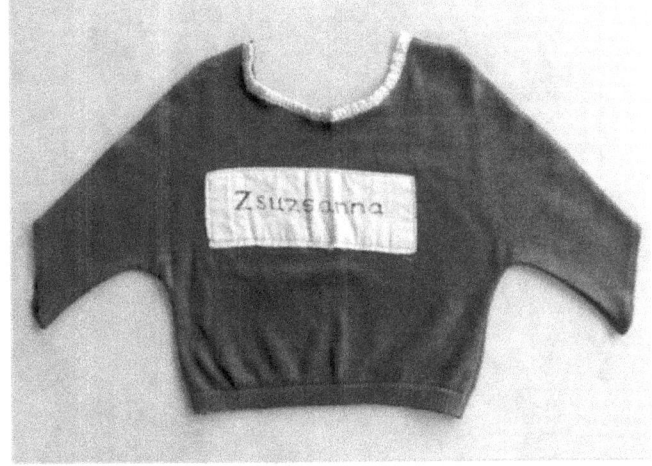

Above: I visit the site of my grandparents' house in Papa with Mr. Laszlo Kiss in 2002. Earlier we had pored over wartime photos and docos, including the rather chilling Auschwitz transportation document that had my name on it.

Right: a copy of the sweater I was wearing when my parents found me in the cattle barn after the Siege of Budapest. I use it to dramatic effect during my school talks!

Above: Chatting to Queensland Premier Annastacia Palasczczuk in October 2022 after she announced the creation of a $7.5m Holocaust Museum in Brisbane.

Right: Being inspired by 100-year-old Holocaust survivor Bert Klug at the Museum announcement event.

Bottom right: Meeting with the Israeli Ambassador, Amir Maimon, in Brisbane 2022.

Above: Schmoozing with my beautiful friend Phyllis in Noosa, still best buds after forty years.

Middle: Catching up with the dynamic Brigitte Gabriel in Washington DC.

Bottom: With former PM John Howard in 1996.

Teaching future generations about the Holocaust ... here I am delivering one of my regular Courage to Care presentations to a school in Brisbane.

CONCLUSION

Never ever, ever again

IF YOU are reading this, the chances are you've ploughed through the preceding thirty chapters of my topsy-turvy, traumatic life – warts and all. Thank you for your patience and perseverance.

For me at least, it was an incredible journey – researching the big historical picture alongside my co-writer Terry Quinn, a journalist and author, and renewing contact with many long-lost people from my past to ferret out snippets of information pertaining to my family story. But it also seemed surreal at times to be sitting in quiet comfort at my Noosa home while looking back at the horrors of the Holocaust when destruction, disease and death were the devastating daily realities of life for my fellow Jews.

Perversely, I felt I could almost understand the deniers, those deluded morons who say it never happened. Why? Because the magnitude of the evil, of the diabolical scheming and cold-blooded machinations designed to kill a whole race of people, was in itself unbelievable.

My primary reason for writing this memoir was, and is, the same one that drove me to get involved with Courage to Care – I want to help keep the memories of what happened during the Holocaust alive for present and future generations. Now in my eightieth year, it was also an opportunity to look back over the events and developments that shaped me as a person. I did so with a mixture of disbelief and wonderment ... at all the drama, the lucky escapes, the ponderous cloud of oppression that hung over everything, first from Nazis, then the communists. And the constant fear and feeling of insecurity that haunted our every thought and deed, as it still haunts me today.

Yet I am so much more blessed than most of my fellow Hungarian Jews. And that is because of several reasons: I escaped being sent to Auschwitz and all its attendant horrors; I survived being 'lost' in the countryside while the Siege of Budapest raged; I reached freedom in Austria in the back of Russian military mail truck; and because I was able to make a new life in the Lucky Country that, after a few false starts, was rich and fulfilling. I struck third time lucky in my choice of husbands. And I was able to forge a rewarding career after a few dispiriting jobs.

During my reflections, I was constantly reminded of all the millions of my fellow Jews, in particular the young ones, whose lives were brutally cut short before they were able to truly experience any of these things – love and joy and fulfilment. Murdered by a vile regime that, even when the war looked lost, carried on relentlessly butchering innocent people whose only 'crime' was that they were Jewish. As an ancient Greek historian once said: "The strong do whatever they want, the weak suffer what they must."

As the history unfolded on these pages, it often struck me that if I were writing fiction rather than a memoir, I could not have conjured up any more unbelievable, unspeakable scenes of inhumanity, some of which I have attempted to describe previously in this story. It was evil enough that the Reich was hell bent on exterminating us, but they also did everything in their power and imagination to humiliate, torture and brutalise us first.

The Nazis took my grandparents and other Jews from their homes and rounded them up in ghettoes; they squashed them into filthy cattle trucks with little food and water; when they arrived in the camps, they killed the young, the weak and the old in the gas chambers; and for those who dodged the ovens – there was starvation, beatings and so-called "medical experiments". In addition, they dreamt up a million different ways to show their contempt for innocent people they considered 'untermensch', or sub-human in the Third Reich's twisted racial philosophy.

With the distance of time, it is easy to scoff and say, it couldn't happen again. But it *is* happening. Not, admittedly, on the scale of the Holocaust. But genocidal persecution is still in evidence around the world. To Uyghurs. To African tribes. To the Rohinga in Myanmar. And to dissidents in many countries. It seems to me that, cometh the hour, cometh the psychopathic despot. In the eighty years since Hitler ignited the Holocaust, a host of other so-called strongmen like Stalin, Mao Zedong, Pol Pot, Idi Amin, Saddam Hussein and Kim Jon-un have emerged, each happy to kill tens of thousands, if not millions, to achieve their diabolical ends.

At the time of writing, Chinese leader Xi Jinping has designs on Taiwan, while Vladimir Putin has invaded Ukraine, despite the objections and sanctions of the western powers. The fact that Ukraine's leader, Volodymyr Yelensky, is Jewish and many members of his family were killed during the Holocaust, makes it even more poignant to me. Familiar pictures of distressed and dispossessed people and burnt-out buildings dominated the TV news channels with children being murdered and women being raped. The shocking scenario in Kyiv reminded me of the Hungarian Uprising when Russian tanks returned to Budapest to crush resistance. My mother had taken in several young refugees when we were living in Kingsford, and they told us of the Russian brutality that had ensued.

And let's not forget that anti-Semitism failed to die with the defeat of Hitler's Germany. Today, if anything, it appears to be on the increase ... in the US, in Europe, and even here in Australia. Synagogues attacked. Holocaust deniers spreading vitriol on social media. Jews continually harassed and abused in the Middle East. Jewish cemeteries desecrated.

According to a European Commission survey, fifty per cent of Europeans consider anti-Semitism a problem in their respective countries, including majorities in Sweden, France, Germany, the Netherlands, the UK, Italy, Belgium and Austria. It also reported that an overwhelming majority of Jews felt that anti-Semitism had risen strongly in Europe since 2013. As Holocaust survivor Elie Wiesel said: "Once I thought anti-Semitism had ended; today it is clear to me that it will probably never end."

Shamefully, even the country of my birth has not learned the lessons of the Holocaust: Hungary has constantly equivocated over the wartime persecution of its Jews, and its authoritarian prime minister, Viktor Orban now presides over a right-wing, nationalist government described by some as "soft-fascist". It has curtailed press freedom, cracked down on migrants and opposed gay rights; it has also been accused of anti-Semitism.

It's not just the shaven-headed, swastika-tattooed right-wing neo-Nazis who are responsible for the recent upsurge; the political Left has also been guilty of virulent anti-Jewish sentiment, particularly since Israel has grown to become a strong, independent, democratic country. Witness the UN's singling out of Israel for alleged human rights abuses, while other known offenders like China and Iran are given a free pass; and take Britain's Labour Party which was the subject of a 2020 report by the UK human rights watchdog that found it guilty of 'unlawful acts' of anti-Semitic harassment and discrimination under the leadership of Jeremy Corbyn, who was then shadow prime minister.

Then there is the everyday casual anti-Semitism demonstrated by people who should know better – like American rapper Kanye West and Hollywood actress Whoopi Goldberg who said on television that the Holocaust was 'not about race'. Even Robert F. Kennedy Junior, who should know better, said when talking about Covid restrictions, that things were worse for people today than they were for Anne Frank, the teenager who died in Bergen-Belsen after hiding from the Nazis in an Amsterdam attic for two years. Perhaps these celebrities could learn something from this old Yiddish proverb: "The wise man, even when he holds his tongue, says more than the fool when he speaks."

All of this explains why, in my eightieth year, I have written this memoir. It is also why I continue spreading the Courage to Care message to schools and other community groups. As Elie Wiesel said: "What hurts the victim most is not the cruelty of the oppressor, but the silence of the bystander."

Nothing illustrates this more compellingly than the opening scene in the 1990 film *Good Evening Mr Wallenberg* made by Swedish director Kjell Grede. The hero diplomat, played by Stellan Skarsgard, is on a train bound for Budapest to begin his mission when it suddenly stops. Wallenberg looks out of the dining car window and observes another train standing stationery on an opposite track. To his horror, soldiers are throwing the corpses of dead Jews from a cattle car. One is a little boy and when his father jumps down to cradle his dead son, he witnesses the soldiers shooting him too. This is Wallenberg's brutal introduction to the Hungarian Holocaust. To his horror, everyone else on his train carries on as if nothing had happened. Nobody says anything about it.

Well, I refuse to be silent. And, for as long as I have left on this earth, I will, in my small way, continue to highlight the evil acts of the Nazis, but also celebrate the good deeds of those like Raoul Wallenberg, Carl Lutz and others who DID do their best to stop the annihilation. And there were many like them: since 1963, nearly twenty-eight thousand people have been awarded the title 'Righteous Among the Nations' for their heroics; their names can be found on the Wall of Honour in the Garden of the Righteous at *Yad Vashem* in Jerusalem. In March 2022, I had the privilege of being asked to speak at a ceremony in Brisbane commemorating just two such brave souls from the Netherlands – Hendrik and Pietertje Bakker, that was hosted by the Israeli Ambassador to Australia, Amir Maimon.

Indeed, this whole project has been an emotionally exhausting rollercoaster ride as I have relived old, forgotten memories, and dug up new facts and pieces of my past. As a young child, I was not developed emotionally or mentally enough to understand what was happening, but I felt the extreme stress, anxiety and helplessness. Indeed, but the blurred and indistinct images and feeling from my childhood still haunt me from time to time, as do the occasional inexplicable panic attacks like the time a few years ago when a black-clad policeman pulled me over at a random breath test checkpoint in Sydney. He wore a peaked cap and leather boots.

Although I had not been drinking, I froze when the cop stooped down and stared in through the window; I suddenly could not breathe or talk. He was pleasant enough and asked me if I was alright. But I couldn't speak, and John took me home. It took some time for me to recover my wits. It is my certain belief that the panic attack was due to some repressed early childhood memory involving an SS officer back in Budapest or Papa.

Looking back, I think I suffered from insecurity until I was forty and met John. After all the stress and trauma of my childhood in wartime Budapest, followed by the communist suppression, the desperate flight to first Austria, and then Australia, and later two marriages to men who did not provide the emotional support I required, there was a certain fragility about my existence that I did not fully appreciate at the time.

Only now, after a further forty years of love, stability and support from John can I identify those symptoms. The difficult relationship with my father throughout my life had not helped, although I accept there was fault on both sides. Prior to John, the only unconditional love came from my darling mother, nyugodjon békében – may she rest in peace.

As I put down these final words to this story, having immersed myself for the last year or so in the harrowing wartime history of my country of birth, I am left with any number of imponderables. Here are just a few:

1. Could/should the Jews have done more to resist? Only a small number of young Hungarian Zionists took the fight to the Nazis. Most other Jews were either ignorant of what was looming or simply resigned to their fate. Perhaps the slow but inexorable trickle of anti-Jewish decrees and repressive regulations prevented them from realising that the outcome was likely to be Endlosung ... the Final Solution. Like the frog in the pot with the water being heated very slowly, by the time it realises it is being boiled alive, it's too late to hop out.

2. Why did the Nazis pursue their heinous annihilation programme to the bitter end, even when it was clear they were losing the war and needed the vast resources expended on killing Jews to be diverted to other fronts? One can only surmise that they were so caught up in their bitter hatred, they could not deviate from this perverted path.

3. Why did more ordinary Hungarians not speak up, or act in support of their fellow citizens who happened to be of a different faith? All the evidence points to the opposite: that many, particularly the Arrow Cross were enthusiastic participants, and even the ones who merely stood on the sideline displayed different degrees of schadenfreude at the fate of the Jews. And, ever since, Hungary's role in the Shoah has been disgracefully whitewashed. Today, a museum in Budapest dedicated to the Holocaust, *The House of Fates*, remains unopened because of conflicting views over whether its themes and exhibits properly reflect Hungarian culpability. *Yad Vashem*, for example, has condemned the museum's content as a falsification of history.

All that said, I am not left feeling bitter, nor am I seeking 'nakam' – vengeance. As Neal Quillinan, the Brisbane teacher who I mentioned earlier had sent me a note after one of my school presentations, said: "The students marvelled at your joyful demeanour, your resilience and complete lack of vindictiveness."

His Excellency Amir Maimon told me recently that, despite all we have suffered, we should view the world in a positive light. And he should know because out of the ashes of the Holocaust, the Jews have created the only true democratic country in the Middle East, and one that has, and continues to contribute so much to the betterment of mankind.

I do believe my cup is half-full, thanks in no small part to the people who helped save me and my family during the war: Janos Okolichny, Samu Stern, Borbola and Zsofia, George Olah and 'Aunt Juliska'.

I continue to pray for an end to the centuries-old venom and vilification directed at the Jewish people. And I also pray that, by a process of education and enlightenment, those who shrivel their spirits in this way can change for the better. The Brisbane Holocaust Museum due to be opened in early 2023 will help with that education. The more visitors to that establishment who learn that unfounded hatred and bigotry can lead to unspeakable acts of inhumanity, the better the world will become.

As Primo Levi says: "An enemy who sees the error of his ways ceases to be an enemy." Or, as I always simply say at the end of my Courage-to-Care talks to schools and other community groups: *'Never again.'*

CHRONOLOGY OF THE HOLOCAUST

1933

January 30 – Adolf Hitler appointed Chancellor of Germany.

March 22 – Dachau concentration camp established.

April 1 – Nationwide boycott of Jewish-owned businesses in Germany, organised by Nazis.

May 10 – Nazi party members, students, professors and others burn books written by Jews.

1935

September 15 – 'Nuremberg Laws' introduced, stripping Jews of German citizenship and forbidding them to marry people of 'pure German blood'.

1937

July 15 – Buchenwald concentration camp established.

October 25 – Hitler and Mussolini form Rome-Berlin axis.

1938

March 12 – Germany annexes Austria to the Third Reich.

November 9-10 – "Kristallnacht", state-organised attacks on Jewish businesses, synagogues, apartments across Germany and Austria.

November 12-15 – German Jews forbidden to pursue their professions, forced to close businesses and assets confiscated.

1939

August 23 – Soviet Union, Germany sign Ribbentrop-Molotov Non-Aggression Pact.

September 1 – German troops invade Poland.

September 3 – Britain and France declare war on Germany.

September 27-28 – Warsaw, home to 350,000 Jews, surrenders to German troops after three-week siege.

October 12 – Germany begins deportation of Austrian and Czech Jews to Poland.

October 28 – The first Jewish ghetto in Poland established in Piotrkow.

November 23 – Yellow Star badge sewn on clothing mandatory for Jews in occupied Poland.

1940

April 9-June 22 Germany invades Denmark, Norway, Belgium, Luxembourg, Holland and France.

May 20 – Auschwitz-Birkenau concentration camp is established outside the Polish city of Oswiecim.

November 15 – German authorities order Warsaw ghetto to be sealed off.

November 20 – Hungary becomes fourth member of the Axis powers alongside Germany, Italy and Japan.

1941

June 22 – German troops invade Soviet Union and are followed by death squads (Einsatzgruppen) that massacre over a million Jews.

July 31 – Reinhard Heydrich, head of the Security Police and the SD (Security Service) ordered to implement the 'Final Solution'.

September 3 – Zyklon-B, a poisonous gas, used for first time to mass murder Soviet prisoners at Auschwitz-Birkenau.

September 29-30 – 33,000 Jews massacred at Babi Yar, on the outskirts of Kiev.

December 7 – Japan bombs Pearl Harbor, Hawaii.

December 8 – The United States declares war on Japan.

1942

January 20 – Guidelines for the implementation of the "Final Solution" established at meeting in Wannsee, organised by Adolf Eichmann.

March 27 – Germany begins systematic deportation of Jews from France, mostly to Auschwitz-Birkenau.

May – Killing in gas chambers begins at Sobibor death camp.

May 4 – SS officials perform first selection of Jewish prisoners for gassing at Auschwitz.

1943

February 2 – German army surrenders at Stalingrad, a major turning point in World War II.

April 19-May 16 – Jewish fighters resist the German attempt to liquidate the Warsaw Ghetto – first mass armed revolt in Nazi-occupied Europe.

August 2 – Jews at Treblinka death camp revolt, using weapons stolen from SS guards.

October 14 – Armed revolt at Sobibor death camp. After recapture and murder of most of the escapees, camp is closed and dismantled.

1944

March 15 – Adolf Hitler lures Hungarian Regent Miklos Horthy to a meeting in Salzburg.

March 19 – Horthy returns to Budapest to find German troops have occupied Hungary. Adolf Eichmann, the architect of the 'Final Solution' arrives in Budapest to begin extermination of Hungary's 800,000 Jews.

March 20 – Eichmann orders creation of Hungarian Judenrat – Jewish Council.

April 5 – Hungary's Jews required to wear yellow star.

May 24 – Papa ghetto established.

May 15-July 9 – The SS, aided by Hungarian rural gendarmes, deport more than 430,000 Jews from Hungary to Auschwitz.

June 6 – British and American troops launch D-Day invasion in Normandy.

June 30 – The "Kasztner Train" leaves Budapest with more than 1600 Jews bound for Switzerland.

July 7 – Hungarian Regent Miklos Horthy stops transportation of Hungarian Jews to Auschwitz.

July 9 – Raoul Wallenberg arrives in Budapest to begin heroic work of saving city's Jews.

July 23 – Soviet troops liberate Majdanek death camp and find evidence of mass murder.

October 16 – Ferenc Szalasi and fascist party, the Arrow Cross seize power in Hungary with German assistance.

November 8 – More than 70,000 Jews—men, women, and children – herded into Ujlaki brickyards in Obuda, and then forced to march on foot to camps in Austria.

November 29 – Budapest ghetto established.

November 1944-January 1945 – Arrow Cross fascists randomly grab thousands of Jews and take them to Danube embankment and shoot them into the river.

December 24 – The siege of Budapest begins.

1945

January 21-26 – Nazis blow up the gas chambers and crematoria in Auschwitz-Birkenau.

January 27 – Red Army liberates Auschwitz-Birkenau.

February 13 – The Siege of Budapest ends.

April 11-29 – Allied troops liberate death camps of Buchenwald, Bergen-Belsen and Dachau.

April 30 – Hitler commits suicide in his bunker in Berlin.

May 7-9 – German armed forces surrender unconditionally.

24 September – Japan surrenders. World War II is officially over.

November 20 – International Military Tribunal convenes in Nuremberg, Germany. Twenty-two top Nazi leaders stand trial for crimes against humanity and war crimes. All plead not guilty.

Post-war

June 8, 1946 – Samu Stern, president of the Hungarian Judenrat, dies.

October 20, 1946 – Ten Nazis including former German Foreign Minister Joachim von Ribbentrop are hanged. Hitler's deputy Hermann Goring committed suicide days before execution.

May 14, 1948 – The State of Israel is established. Jewish immigration is unrestricted, and almost 700,000 are admitted, including more than two-thirds of Jewish displaced persons from Europe.

March 15, 1957 – Rudolf Kasztner assassinated in Tel Aviv.

April 10, 1961 – Adolf Eichmann put on trial in Israel for Crimes Against Humanity. He is convicted and hanged on June 1, 1962.

ACKNOWLEDGEMENTS

When I set out to write my life story, I had assumed it would end up being a slim volume, perhaps stretching to several hundred words, accompanied by a selection of family photographs and documents, that chronicled my rather colourful eight decades on this planet. Maybe, I thought, it could even become a nicely packaged book that would grace the coffee tables of friends and family. A lasting reminder to them of my journey from Budapest to Noosa, and all points in between.

It was not until my friend and collaborator Terence J. Quinn and I started researching the incredible, gut-wrenching story behind the Hungarian Holocaust that the potential scale of *The Courage to Care* started to emerge.

As a highly-experienced journalist who has worked in several countries, he knew where to look and how to ferret out important facts and crucial documents that I had been unaware even existed. Gradually, it became clear just how entwined my family history was with the remarkable, and largely untold, history of the Nazi occupation of the country of my birth. It was an exhilarating, and often painful process mining the rich seam of personal memories and the often heart-wrenching information about that terrible period in history that is in the public domain. Despite sleepless nights and stressful moments that punctuated the writing of this memoir, I would not have missed the experience for the world. It truly has added a fulfilling new dimension to my twilight years.

Together we looked at hundreds of book extracts, academic papers, shipping manifests, museum archives, websites and sundry other sources of material that informed our output and provided astonishing background details to my story. Terry's experience as an author helped shape the structure of this memoir, and his writing skills helped make even dense subject matter highly readable. For that, and his unfailing support throughout this literary journey, I thank him from the bottom of my heart.

It is important that we acknowledge the many people, Jews and non-Jews alike, who remain committed to continue shining a light on the Shoah or Holocaust, often at great personal cost. They are truly wonderful human beings. Much of the information we gleaned came from a variety of sources. Not least via the wonderful Wikipedia and Google.

I have tried to list as many as possible below, but of course, I owe my gratitude to many others. These include Noosa people like Suzie Endrey and Tibor Kegye who helped with translation (Hungarian is not an easy language!), to others I have never met such as Anna Sas, Samu Stern's great granddaughter who still lives in Budapest, noted Hungarian historian Krisztian Ungvary and the incredibly helpful Zsolt Zagoni in that same city who acted as an intermediary with the Sas family and also sent me a copy of Stern's book.

Nearer home, old friends and family members (some of whom feature in this book) have contributed relevant information and anecdotes. They include Phyllis O'Brien, still one of my oldest confidantes after more than forty years, my cousin Robert Kalmar and my friend Peter Halas. Thanks also to Peter Hegedus, a Budapest-born film writer, director and producer, now Brisbane-based, who interviewed me on camera for a Holocaust Museum project. Jason Steinberg and Peter Myers of the Queensland Jewish Board of Deputies have provided tremendous encouragement and support.

I also give a huge shout out to my wonderful, dedicated colleagues who provide an invaluable service via the Courage to Care organisation. They include Kayla Szumer in Queensland and Kathy Sharp, the vice chair of the C2C board, who smoothed the way for me to use their very apt name as the title for this book. One of the joys of my work with Courage to Care is that it brings me into contact with other wonderful people that I would not otherwise have come to know, including other courageous Holocaust survivors, and the victims of other injustices.

Despite my humble and traumatic beginnings in Hungary, nowadays I am proud to know many high-profile Aussies such as Gina Rinehart, Alan Jones, and a swag of senior politicians, showbiz personalities and legal luminaries such as Ian Callinan and David Kirby.

I first met Alan Jones, who is arguably Australia's best-known broadcaster, and a former Wallabies coach, in January 2010. He kindly acted as the MC for the opening event in Sydney of an Australia-wide speaking tour that John and I, and others, had organised for Lord Christopher Monckton, the British expert on climate change.

It was the Australia Day weekend, and Lord Monckton, a former adviser to Margaret Thatcher, was supported on the platform by Professor Ian Plimer, the distinguished geologist and professor emeritus at the University of Melbourne. More than 900 people turned up to the presentation at the Sheraton on the Park. Afterwards, Alan treated a group of us, including Christopher and his wife Juliet, to dinner at his beautiful apartment overlooking Sydney Opera House. He has been a good friend ever since.

I have only known Amir Maimon, the warm and inspiring Israeli ambassador to Australia, for a short time, but he has become a wonderful friend, and is tremendously supportive of my efforts. We first met in early 2022, when he invited me to speak at a 'Righteous Among the Nations' event in Brisbane. Since then, I have enjoyed his company, and that of his lovely wife Tal, a few times, in Canberra, and at my home in Noosa. The former paratrooper, a decorated Lieutenant Colonel in the Israeli Defence Force, very generously offered to write the introduction to this book. Toda raba, Amir. Thank you!

I am grateful to Dr Anthony Cappello and his team at Connor

Court Publishing – in particular, editor Michael Gilchrist – who turned my story into a beautiful book, and my dream into reality.

To my parents, my mother in particular, who somehow saved me (and themselves) from certain death, not once but several times. They brought me to this wonderful country of Australia and made me who I am today. I love and miss you both.

And finally, let me pay tribute to 'Aircon Guy' John, my husband and best friend for forty years. He changed my life forever when he wooed and pursued me at a time when I was down, but not out. Since then, he has been my companion and my champion throughout. And, typically, when I embarked on this, at times difficult and exhausting memoir journey, he held my hand and caressed my face. His unconditional love and support have kept me sane. I owe him everything.

SOURCES USED IN THIS MEMOIR

As I stated in the prologue, I am neither a historian nor an academic; that is why I have not included footnotes in the various chapters to reference source material. The following are just some of the people and places that provided critical information about either my family history or the context and of the Hungarian Holocaust itself. My heartfelt thanks go to:

The people at Yad Vashem in Jerusalem and the US Holocaust Centre in Washington DC who were very helpful and generous with archive material.

The Hungarian Historical Review.

JSTOR.org.

Academia.edu.

Professor R.L. Braham – probably the most eminent and quoted Hungarian Holocaust historian.

Andrew J. Chandler – www.chandlerozconsultants.wordpress.com

Jewishgen.org.

The Hungarian Jewish Museum and Archives.

Some of the academic papers, books and monographs that we drew on include:

The Trains of the Holocaust – Hedi Enghelberg.

The Memorial Book of Papa Jewry – Gyula Yehuda Lang.

Occupied Hungary's 1944 Murder Machine – Eszter Edler.

The Mechanics of Murder – Jason Michael McCann.

The Yellow Star and Everyday Life under Exceptional Circumstances: Diaries of 1944-1945 Budapest – Louise O. Vasvari.

The Dissemination and Reception of News about Auschwitz in Hungary in 1944 – Gergely Kunt.

Why Should I Care? Lessons from the Holocaust – Jeanette Friedman and David Gold.

Inside the Ghetto: Everyday Life in Hungarian Ghettoes – Regina Fritz.

Hungary in the Second World War: Tragic Blunders or Destiny – Geza Jeszenszky.

The Holocaust in Hungary – Laszlo Karsai.

Altering Alternatives: Mapping Jewish Subcultures in Budapest – Eszter Gantner

Horthy – Andrea Pellicciotti.

The Strange Mr Kastner: A Reappraisal of Rescue Efforts in Holocaust-era Hungary – Paul Sanders.

The Experiences of Hungarian Slave and Forced Labourers – Eva Kovacs.

Memory and Justice – Ruth Wodak.

Brief History of the Holocaust – Montreal Holocaust Memorial Centre.

Routledge History of the Holocaust – Jonathan Friedman.

The Concentration and Extermination Camp Auschwitz, History and After-History – Marc Buggeln.

The Role of Public Administration in the Hungarian Holocaust – Eva Gulyas.

The Explanation – Steve Colman.

The Historiography of the Shoah – Marina Cattaruzza.

The Fate of Judaica in Hungary during the Nazi and Soviet Occupations – Zsuzsanna Toronyi.

From Budapest to Bergen-Belsen: A notebook from 1944 – Rosza Bamberger.

My Memoir - Race Against Time! – Samu Stern.

Story of a Budapest Garden – Zsuzsanna Toronyi.

The Ties That Bind: Australia, Hungary and the case of Karoly Zentai – Ruth Balint.

Why Should I care? Lessons from the Holocaust – Jeanette Friedman & David Gold.

ABOUT THE AUTHORS

Suzi Smeed is a Hungarian Holocaust survivor. Born Zsuzsanna Kalmar in Budapest in 1942, she escaped from a ghetto and escaped death three times following the German occupation of Hungary. She and her family fled from Budapest after communist threats, first to Vienna and then to Australia in 1949 where her turbulent life included three marriages and a stint as the star of a TV shopping channel. She now works for the Courage to Care organisation educating school students and community groups about the Holocaust. Her written and video testimony has featured both at Yad Vashem in Jerusalem and the US Holocaust Museum in Washington DC. She has been filmed for the Brisbane Holocaust Museum and interviewed by the ABC and several magazines and newspapers. In 2022, the Israeli ambassador to Australia, Amir Maimon, invited her to address a group of foreign diplomats in Canberra on Holocaust Remembrance Day. Still fit and active at the age of 80, she lives in Noosa.

Terence J. Quinn had a long, successful newspaper career as a journalist, editor and publisher in the UK, US, NZ, Canada, and lastly in Australia where he has lived for 18 years. Along the way, he edited two metropolitan dailies as well as the UK's fifth largest national newspaper, the *Scottish Daily Record*. He was also Editorial Director of three major newspaper chains in the UK, US and Australia/NZ, and publisher of two national Sunday papers in New Zealand. He is a founding committee member of the World Editors Forum and was a regular speaker at international media conferences. He lectured at the American Press Institute in Washington DC and the European School of Journalism. Since 2017, Quinn has written three thrillers, two of which were published by Simon & Schuster. He has been based in Australia since 2004 and now lives in Noosa.

More information: www.terencejquinn.com.au

www.ingramcontent.com/pod-product-compliance
Lightning Source LLC
Chambersburg PA
CBHW070758230426
43665CB00017B/2408